D1253004

the STASH BOOK

How to Hide Your Valuables

Peter Hjersman

And/Or Press
Berkeley • California

Asbury Park Public Library
500 First Avenue
Asbury Park, N.J. 07712

Copyright © 1978 by Peter Hjersman

Published and Distributed by
And/Or Press
P.O. Box 2246
Berkeley, CA 94702

ISBN: 0-915904-34-9
Library of Congress Catalog Card No.: 78-54343

Printed in U.S.A.
First printing 1978

Cover design: Bonnie Smetts
Typesetting: Dick Ellington
Paste-up: Sandy Drooker
Manuscript editors: Aidan Kelly and Marina La Palma

Asbury Park Public Library
500 First Avenue
Asbury Park, N.J. 07712

Contents

Preface

As I began this book, I thought it a simple task. Within two months, I thought, it would be finished. After all, I had just spent two intense years writing and printing my first book. I had learned so much about writing, book design, readability, printing, binding, typography, and more, that I felt competent to lunge into this light, superficial task with my "vast" knowledge and heartfelt experiences. Will learning never cease? As months passed and much searching ensued and hiding places were constructed, I was drawn and encompassed deep within its web. Once my mind began to consider *HIDING*, new sources emerged, and avalanches of experiences poured from every nook and cranny. Discovering the pervasiveness of hiding has been an astounding experience.

The meanings of hiding began to become clear as historical precedents marched forth in review from myriad pages before my questing eyes: the Underground Railroad before our Civil War, the old spies of Japan, the hidden corridors and rooms in castles and palaces. It became clear that hiding is far more a part of our lives than had ever occurred to me. It courses in a natural flow through all we do.

As the book progressed, I saw that I had been making the almost universal assumption that there is something negative about hiding and secrecy. As this lesson struck deep within, I became dissatisfied. Why is hiding so negative? Fear was the only answer I could find, and my dissatisfaction continued. I wracked my brain, but I could find nothing to release me from the idea of hiding as negative. Then, at last, slowly, slowly, I saw the transition: from fear *TO* something else. Now, with this direction in hand, I remembered playing hide-and-seek; I remembered building secret forts and tree houses, and searching for the key my father hid for the tool box! Then I saw that the fear is balanced by *JOY*! The *JOY*, the fun of secret worlds, popped into my mind, redirected my writing energy; the balance was now apparent!

After these stages, the challenge became to decide which items to hone and polish for the book. Many incredible stories and rumors did not have a sound basis, and some hiding is best left deep within. Yet the joy of hiding continues, whether it is occasionally concealed or not! To see the *JOY OF HIDING* gives us a greater ease of living, day to day, moment to moment!

There is a secret place
in everyone's heart.

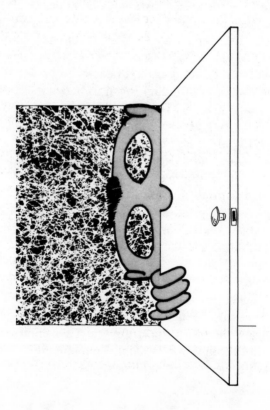

Introduction: The Joy of Hiding

Ever dreamed of being invisible? Or finding a treasure trove? How about the Invisible Pirate? No? Well, dreams, fantasies, daydreams will always be with us. Did you ever play hide-and-seek? Go on a treasure hunt? Children have a marvelous time with endless ideas about secret hidings! The hidden daydreamer evolves in us as children, as fantasies tickle our inner being.

Did you ever dream about making a hidden retreat in your childhood bedroom? A trapdoor on the closet floor which leads to a maze of underground tunnels and rooms, and opens into the neighboring horse pasture or behind a bush? Ever listen to the mice in the wall and dream of walking around inside the walls yourself? Mary Norton's friends *lived* in the walls and under the floor! And what better way to learn all about the construction of the wall than to be a studious mouse pondering this hollow world while tramping around inside?

If you ever need ideas about how to keep a treasure from human eyes, watch children, observe their ways of hiding from friends, teachers, and parents! If an exuberantly cooperative youth graces your day, venture to ask, in a childlike manner, how to hide things. Ask children how they would hide your treasure in your room. Sound crazy? Then you have never consulted their youthful thoughts! Such deep wisdom can emerge . . . but from where? They have not even been in school yet. To draw on children's unrestricted imagination can be a startling experience. Their inventiveness carries astounding weight as they snuggle into an invisible world, vanish under a corner table in their school library, build tunnels and caves by draping blankets over assembled

1

chairs and tables, read with a flashlight under their covers after being put to bed . . .

How many ways can you think of to play hide-and-seek? In a small room with lots of players, turn out the lights. The seeker must find the hiders as they hang from the molding at the top of the walls, balance atop the bedposts, and scramble to places that would not be hidden with the light on: a classic example of misdirecting. And when the seeker finds a person? The hider must be identified by name! The same can be done in a swimming pool at night or in the sun with the seeker's eyes closed. Does it ever end? Ask them! And then really look at yourself.

Walter Mitty will never lose his pervading visions, as he adapts to every situation that comes his way and pumps it full with his dreams. Sherlock Holmes uncovered a vast range of concealed motives and hiding places as he pursued imaginative hiders. H.G. Wells' *Invisible Man* discovered the advantages of being invisible! With our fantasies we can both hide from reality and pleasantly explore our potential. All our dreams are hidden fantasies until they come true. Being invisible is a threat-free position, in which we have nothing to lose, nothing to fear: is not hiding being invisible? Do not our hidden valuables vanish before our eyes, as they cuddle into their secure nest? Is not hiding a fantasy? Are our possessions really something someone would steal? Or is it just important for us to think so? Sometimes we make sure we have something worth stealing to increase our own self-worth. If we build a secret cache, then we *must* have something that is worth stealing—if not, we will obtain something we value. Of course, a burglar would never be tempted by a poor man's house, nor would the tax collector!

How many efforts draw on our love of hiding? Our libraries abound with mystery stories. Fantasy books range from *The Borrowers* through heroes and heroines seeking long-lost magic rings, or a treasure, or hidden cities. Myths and folklore pass on adventurous centuries of searching for lost treasures and people. To everyone's delight, fairy tales expose our common dreams. Besides literary epics, other endeavors, such as science, art, philosophy, and religion, excite us with their profound seeking and answers.

Hiding exists all about us. We float in the hidden river and often lose our footing. How can hiding be so common to all people? It is a great mystery—and *THAT* is why we hide! In all we do, we seek the answer to the mystery of life, our feelings and experiences, and we find that *WE ARE AS BIG A MYSTERY AS ALL OTHER LIFE*!

We balance the *Joy of Hiding* with its inhererent *Joy of Seeking!* Even children hide and then seek each other in their play. Philosophy verbalizes our guesses about the vast, unknown, unreached, hidden world about us. Science is our logical study of the unknown. The secrets of life evade us and all our efforts. From this science has emerged. Art expresses our unlimited feeling about the unseen, about our search for understanding our daily lives. It explores that secret part of our being, expresses our feelings, and shares many rich experiences.

To see and feel the widespread existence of hiding in all we do, every second of our lives, is to find *joy* in life as it is. To enjoy our secrets and our hidden valuables frees us from hiding out of fear and makes it fun. Consider the enjoyment in children's games, and how the feeling of joy in having something hidden tells us of the positive side of secrets.

So what *is* hiding? Hiding is a conscious intent to actively conceal. Conceal oneself, one's feelings, one's valuables—but do not conceal the Joy! We are ever wondering about the secret possibilities around us; objects can be hidden anywhere.

Magic is a delightful outcome of our love of hiding. The "art of illusion" uses the concept of misdirection to tempt our interest with unseen enchantments. Houdini, Blackstone, Thurston—these were masters of directing our attention away from one object or action and toward another. Techniques and apparatus used by these charming illusionists offer—to the properly prepared—a wide range of ways to conceal objects.

Buried treasures can be found anywhere: a jar of gold dust at the beach; gold coins and diamonds inside a tree; buried tin cans filled with money; safes from shipwrecks that lie on the bottom of the sea; lost gold and silver mines; treasure-laden ships from the discovery of America—a farmer may even plough up old coins! To tramp around the beach or an empty site with a metal detector is a much-enjoyed hobby.

We find joy in a vacation in a mountain cabin, a sailboat on the sea, a retreat to a private haven. What about visiting ghost towns and seeking lost civilizations? Hiding pervades all of life and blends vast joy with us.

HIDDEN AND HIDING

Throughout our lives we find hidden places and hiding places. A *hidden* place is a secret place that is visually out of sight of probing eyes. To build a hidden room or cubbyhole is to *screen* the searcher's vision. This is one approach, often the most appropriate, and the one usually suspected by people who are seeking hidden goods. Move about your house and discover hidden places under the stairs, a small panel in the backroom, a concealed wine cellar.

A *hiding* place uses an understanding of human nature to protect valuables from being found. This is the same *misdirecting* of energy used in magic. It takes less physical energy, but more creative energy.

Once we begin to comprehend these two approaches—screening and misdirecting—and conceive of ways to use them, to know when and where each is appropriate, and actually to execute some of these ideas, then we can begin to conceive of our spaces in new ways. A wall is no longer an impenetrable barrier; a piece of furniture becomes a *dynamic* part of our fixtures; a room is no longer *only* what it seems! An entirely new awareness awaits those who explore their spaces, who reach into hidden corners and buried fantasies, and bring life into their hidden, secret selves. We can learn about our openness by exploring our hiding!

In "The Purloined Letter," Edgar Allan Poe clearly discusses these two approaches and shows how they are used, both by hiders and seekers. The story unfolds a deep exploration of hiding.

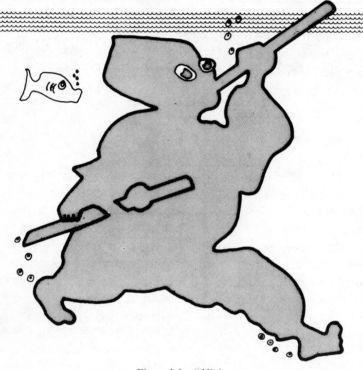

Figure 1.1. A Ninja.

Stash Past

Throughout history there have been many times when capable hiding and secreting were necessary to survival, such as during the American Civil War, Prohibition, and the return of the Catholics to sixteenth-century England. A study of such precedents can be very useful to the serious hider.

SECRET AGENTS

One of the most totally concealed groups in history was the *ninja* of feudal Japan. Their entire lives were based on hiding! From the thirteenth to the seventeenth century, a period of strife and transition, ninja families aided the regional rulers. The Japanese soldiers, the samurai, lived by a very strict code. The ninja filled the holes the samurai left: secret assassinations, stealing and delivering documents, spying, all the hidden and undercover activities needed during war.

Training began at about the age of three, when a purchased child was brought into the clan. These boys and girls were prepared to cope with any situation, even the totally unexpected. Their physical stamina, mental ability, and skill in every martial art were highly developed. In their homes, they learned to use concealed floor levels, spy holes in corners, underground escape tunnels.

The hidden, secret life of the ninja was not simply a side interest; it was the *basis* of their entire lives, for both men and women. They had a public life, often more than one, plus their secret life. In their work they dressed entirely in black, for much of their work was done at night. In the snow? During winter, they wore white outfits! A ninja house still exists

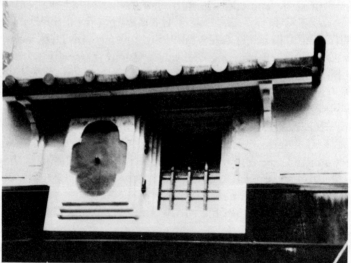

Figure 1.2. Japanese *kura* were built to store treasured items, and often had thick walls and special windows.

in Iga-Ueno, Japan, and is maintained as a museum with sample costumes and a wide variety of their tools. The ninja dealt not merely with hiding or delivering government documents or with secret assassinations; every monent of their lives was spent hiding their true vocations and their secret missions! For their work, they learned extreme diets, such as extended fasting, carrying small quantities of food that would last them for long periods, even going without water. Techniques of regathering strength similar to ancient Tibetan and Indian methods were used. They became so influential that even the castles built during their time reflected the inhabitants' desire to keep the ninja at bay. In one castle in Kyoto, if anyone steps on specially made floors, a sound alerts the guards.

The ninja used ingenuity in all their tools and weapons. They used every conceivable method to fully develop their *inpo,* the art of hiding! They learned to hide themselves so well that legends say they could fly, walk on water, disappear at will, walk through castle walls, and turn into animals. Their many methods led to these stories. They used the guard on their sword for a ladder. The scabbard had a hole in the bottom to allow them to breathe while hiding underwater. They hid a variety of weapons all over themselves, and their homes were a web of hidden spaces.

Other governments have used agents with superstealth, although none as developed as ninja. The United States has used the Federal Bureau of Investigation since 1908 and the Central Intelligence Agency since 1947. The agents continue to use inventive methods of concealment and seeking operations for national security.

THE UNDERGROUND

During any war an underground resistance evolves to counteract the occupation. In *The Hiding Place,* Corrie ten

Boom shares her experiences during World War II, when she worked with the underground in Holland. A hidden room in her family's home was the city's center for concealing fleeing Jews. At the same time, Anne Frank lived in a secret room for two years, as described in *Diary of a Young Girl.* During her concert tours, the dynamic French singer Edith Piaf smuggled false papers to captured French soldiers, by concealing their papers in a double-bottomed makeup case. Resistance activities rely heavily on appropriate uses of numerous hiding places.

Before the split in our nation from 1861 to 1865, the *Underground Railroad* was developed to create a path to freedom for the slaves. It was a loosely bound group of abolitionists who *conducted passengers* to the North by hiding them in *stations* and giving them false travel documents. Houses which served as stations had secret rooms, passages, and trapdoor entries. Loaded carts and disguises were also used. Operating from about 1810 to 1850, the Railroad moved an estimated 100,000 slaves out of the South. Around 1850, slave owners began to tire of this migration. They hassled, arrested, imprisoned, and sometimes killed the Railroad conductors. Laws were passed, but abolitionists continued to strengthen their hidden efforts until the war itself broke out.

Relatively few years later, a law was passed which brought a new use of hiding places in our country: Prohibition! Since this change affected such a wide cross section of our population, an amazing diversity of stash spots was used. During the fourteen years that Prohibition lasted, 1919–1933, in homes and later in commerce, liquors were stashed. False bottoms and holds in boats and fishing vessels carried some beverages. Even the Coast Guard was not immune. One crew smuggled 150 *hams* (six bottles per ham) of liquor aboard and had a tremendous revelry, while the captain and his officers ransacked the ship to find the contraband. They were on the verge of giving up—when the captain decided to take a drink of water. Being a resolute teetotaler, he recoiled at the first taste. The water tank had been drained of water, and all the bottles emptied into it!

A method called *trapping* was used by fishermen. On their way to the fishing grounds, they passed through the off-shore "Rum Row," where *contact boats* awaited them outside the territorial limits. Their bottled cargo was sold to the fishermen, who then covered it with their catch. Trapping is an old smuggling dodge, dating back to the Napoleonic wars, when smugglers in the Narrow Seas gave the British Coast Guard of their era a bad time with brandy, lace, tobacco, and other contraband. Trapping uses secret compartments stashed under a ship's false bilge or the bottom of the hull.

A rather different type of underground is to live under the earth. Cave living harks back to our ancient ancestors, who lived in caves and huddled around the fire to keep away their carnivorous neighbors.

In Fresno, California, Baldasare Forestiere dug out seven acres underground by hand, which included some area for fruit trees, his home, and a tunnel for cars to his restaurant! While he dug, between 1908 and 1946, he managed to stash in his underground maze a still for his brother's grapes. The FBI could never find this still, even after numerous searches.

Figure 1.3. *Left:* Fresno underground gardens: entrance. *Right:* Fruit tree in underground courtyard.

Once Prohibition was over, the agents returned and asked to be shown where the still was. When they saw how easy it was to find, they were rather amazed at Forestiere's skill in keeping it hidden!

Even architects are beginning to build underground. They have begun to realize the joy of experiencing the closeness of the earth. There are practical reasons to build under the ground. Properly designed, underground homes can save tremendous amounts of energy, and can cut out most outside noises—from traffic, for example. The new ground level can be replanted to provide new living places for animals and birds.

RELIGIOUS SECRETS

Every religion uses hidden doctrines, attitudes, and places. Orthodox Jews, following Deuteronomy 6:4–9 and 11:13–21, place a small wooden, metal, or glass case at the upper right section of the doorpost of each room. This case, called a *mezuzah,* is about three inches long and contains parchment inscribed with fifteen verses from the Torah. Sometimes it is placed on the outside of the doorway, visible to the eye, but the parchment is still stashed inside the often beautiful case. During construction, the case is sometimes placed under the finished surface, and even though hidden from view, the hidden blessing still remains.

Buddhists often place a roll of prayer in statues of the Buddha. It may be placed in the back, hidden behind a panel, in the arm, or in a hole drilled in the bottom of the statue.

The early Christians used the underground catacombs in their cities and caves in the countryside for meeting places, as did many other groups at the time. The fish symbol, still seen today, guided fellow Christians to these meeting places. Even the stories they heard, parables in the Bible, voiced covert moral attitudes in a manner enjoyable to all ages.

In the Vatican Museum in Rome, Catholics maintain a

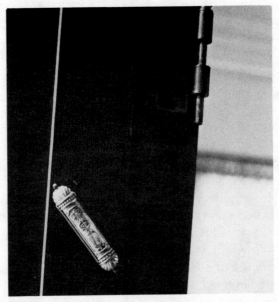

Figure 1.4. Mezuzah (display courtesy of Isaac Kikawada).

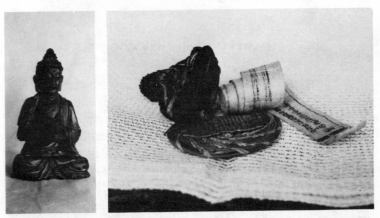

Figure 1.5. The smiling Buddha hides a hand-printed scroll of prayers. (From the collection of Hanny Berglund.)

vast collection of ancient books, inventions, and other treasures that are not available for public viewing. Amazing rumors allude to profound wealth and secrets stored in their vaults!.

In England, there was a long struggle between Protestants and Catholics. Queen Elizabeth, who reigned from 1558 to 1603, officially banned Catholicism, removed the Pope's authority from England, prohibited the mass, and required compulsory attendance at Protestant services. As the devout priests continued their work and the Jesuits were formed, they used disguises, acted roles, and built and used secret chapels, mass centers, and places to hide, sometimes called "priest's holes." Nicholas Owen, an architect, mason, and carpenter became a Jesuit. He spent 18 years constructing hiding places of all kinds. He became well-known for his unlimited ingenuity, yet only a few of his works remain today. John Gerard, one of the "hunted priests," details his and Owen's work in *The Autobiography of a Hunted Priest.* Under King James I, Owen was finally betrayed, tortured, and executed. He never revealed the numerous hidden centers he knew nor the whereabouts of the priests.

CASTLES AND PALACES

European castles and palaces abound with stash places. During civil strife in the Middle Ages in Europe, the people needed strong protection. The castles became nearly cities in themselves, with many secret meetings and frequent hiding of people. Catherine de Medici had hidden wall panels in her Italian palace. Maria Theresa had a secret passage from the council room in her palace in Vienna to the chancellor's rooms above. Mont St. Michel's barely lit defensive spiral staircases have sudden pitfalls where a step should have been— to discourage a fast pursuer. After 1500, the fire power of cannons and artillery made such castles obsolete.

Figure 1.6. European castles have secret doors (Hellbrunn Castle, Salzburg, Austria; photo by Kosaku Wada) and isolated locations (Pfalz Castle, Germany).

Figure 2.1.

The Burglar's View

A chat with your neighborhood brigands can enlighten you, the hider, about who they are, how they operate, and how you can prevent their successful exploits.

"I went through a place and couldn't find nothing. And then I spotted a new toaster in the kitchen and I thought, Jees, my old lady needs a toaster, so I took it. When I got home and tried it, nothing happened. Then I looked inside and saw some money. The toaster was a fake, even had a fake slice of bread in it, and was plugged into the wall and everything. If I hadn't needed a toaster, I never would have found the money. It almost worked."

"One time we went through this place and they didn't have a tv or stereo or nothing. But it was a nice place. My buddy searched one room and I took another. I finished and asked if he found anything. He said no. I decided to look myself. The bottom drawer of the dresser, which he'd already checked, was full of purses, big ones, all sizes. I found a small coin purse and inside was a roll of bills, all fifties and hundreds! I don't know, I just had a feeling."

"Most people think the safest place in the world to hide stuff is in your home and in your own special spot. This is the attitude the burglar loves, because wherever it is, he'll find it, given enough time."

"The kitchen . . . you know, it's funny, but women hide things in the kitchen and such, in an empty and carefully closed milk carton in the back of the refrigerator, in an empty

17

can they carefully put the lid back on, and they really do keep money in sugar bowls! Men put valuables in their bowling bags or golf bags, you know, places like that."

"Lots of times I find stuff rolled up in socks, or under mattresses—all the corny old places. People really think these are safe."

"People think that walls and roofs are safe. Roofs are easy. I'll go through the roof of one place, drop down inside, and go through the wall into the place next door. Nobody ever thinks about that."

"If a burglar suspects a hiding place, he'll break it open to get into it. He doesn't care, doesn't cost him nothing."

These incidents are all true. They were all related to me by helpful inmates at San Quentin State Prison in California. One thing they all said, and their ease in talking about their experiences proved, is that burglary is fun. "When you get away, man, and you know that you're not gonna get caught, that's a real good feeling! Even doing the job is exciting; it's a rush, man!" There is an excitement in stealing from someone, a thrill, a challenge in gaining entry and in finding the hidden valuables.

Some burglars have well-developed intuitions and are very sensitive to spatial peculiarities. On a hunch, they will frequently go directly to your most secret hiding place. Even a specially constructed stash place has no assurance of escaping their active imaginations.

There are three basic types of burglars: the grabber, the professional, and the selector. The *grabber* may do no more than run in the door and grab anything he can, maybe just for the thrill of stealing, like a neighborhood kid. He may be a junkie needing something to sell. The grab-and-run types get in and get out fast. They can hit your home while the door is open on a pleasant summer afternoon. Anything near

the door, a radio, a purse, a camera, or anything that would
sell could easily be grabbed. Even stereos or televisions are
grabber targets. These burglars do not have the range of skills
the professionals and selectors have. Usually they are not as
old nor as thorough. Ordinarily they operate quickly; so any
hiding place would probably escape their attention.

The *professional* will choose one type of victim and
study the situation carefully, ascertaining the daily schedule,
and finding out whether or not alarm systems are used. He
will choose a time when he can scour the house without dis-
turbance, sometimes even at night while the occupants are
asleep. He may have the skills to pick locks, open safes, and
enter without breaking anything. He probably has a *fence*
waiting for him when he finishes the job. The fence buys the
goods he has stolen and distributes them. The professional
steals on speculation and takes what he can sell. He does not
have inside information on his victims and probably does not
know what items are in the house. To hide valuables from
this burglar takes skill in hiding, breaking of the daily routine
patterns, and better location of valuables. The professional is
the biggest threat. Although he is less common than the grabber, he is more thorough, more skilled, and better organized.
To hide valuables from his skilled hands and quick mind requires clear thought and appropriate hiding places.

The *selector* is better trained than the professional. The
difference is that he has been directed to a specific house by
someone who wants a specific valuable and may even know
where it is kept. He could be hired to steal a selected painting
for a wealthy collector, or documents for industry or a government. The selector is the most competent and rare type of
burglar. Since he is after a selected piece of merchandise from
one specific house, he is difficult to discourage. If he knows a
house has a special item, he will find it eventually. The best
defense is to provide an unexpected situation for the burglar.
Munro tells how he lifted a jewelry box next to a sleeping victim; when he opened the lid, its music box started to play!

After much careful preparation, Barnes managed to get into a basement of a home to rob the safe, only to find a leopard on top of it! A wee bit of ingenuity can throw a burglar off guard and right out of the house.

Of the steps a burglar goes through, only four concern the occupant directly. These are:

choosing the victim;
gaining entry;*
locating the valuables; and
effecting an escape.

A burglar will usually concentrate on one type of home. This specialization allows him to take advantage of social patterns, such as daily schedules, certain types of valuables in different classes of homes, certain types of hiding places. He depends on uniformity and predictable patterns; uncertainty discourages him. The point here is to break those patterns. If you read the information in this book carefully, it may help you to become aware of your patterns and to break them, throwing uncertainty in the path of any prospective burglars.

Don't rely on luck. Do not count on any burglar's overlooking keys hidden outside or valuables inside. To play roulette against the skills of a burglar is asking for trouble. Burglar-alarm systems can protect a house from prying fingers. They may not totally discourage the determination of the professionals or selectors, but will certainly discourage the grabbers. A stash does not have to be superelaborate or complicated in order to escape the attention of the grabber. Low-energy, high-risk places—the hollow stapler, the fake book—will escape their rapid glances.

In choosing a place to safely stash valuables, the *first*

---

*Usually only doors and windows are considered as points of entry. If a burglar can go right through roofs and walls, then the time comes to consider breaking the patterns inside the home.

place that occurs to you will probably also occur to the burglar. Any place a hider thinks of, someone else can think of and probably will. Try thinking like a burglar, and figure out where *you* would look first if you were looking for someone's cache. Then find another place. Do not use the first place you think of, nor the second. Think about it for awhile. Let your thoughts of numerous possibilities grow until the best one becomes clear. If you hide valuables inside a container for instance, use an old, unattractive article, not a new one. If you use a toaster, use an *old* toaster.

Probably the first thing you should put into your hiding place is this book! If a burglar walks in and spots this book, he will be more likely to look for secret compartments that he otherwise would have missed. He will more easily spot different places and broken patterns, since he will be cued to seek unexpected areas. True, he will momentarily be surprised, but he may just accept it as a challenge to *find* your hiding place.

Figure 2.2.

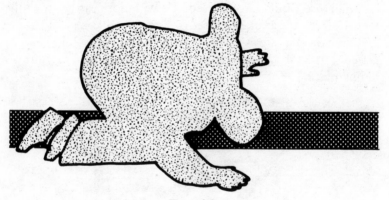

Figure 3.1.

How to Find a Hiding Place

As a start, consider who will be looking for your valuables and decide the energy-risk level that is appropriate. Different methods are required to hide cookies from a child than to hide other valuables from a selector or from a government searcher. The type of valuable must also be considered when choosing a cache. Putting a tape deck in the trunk while doing shopping will probably suffice. Using this technique for smuggling across a border, well, let me know if it *does* work!

Valuables require many types of hiding under myriad circumstances; yet every hiding place can be appropriate for the right conditions. Consider the type of valuable: a rare book, a wealth of jewels, or cash. Consider the type of searcher: burglar or customs. Consider the place of hiding: in the home, in a vehicle, or in a traveler's pocket. To hide cash from grabbers may require no more than a little caution; from professional burglars a well-constructed and well-located concealment may be necessary. To convey contraband across a border requires unfathomable imagination. To secrete an operation such as counterfeiting demands as much ingenuity as undetected smuggling.

The "searcher's mind" must be considered. Review your own experiences of looking for and finding something: cookies as a child, or the key for the cabinet they are locked in. You can easily see that any hollow spot or any object that has some volume is suspect, whether you are checking a cookie jar for cookies, or the inside of a wall for a hidden room or a secret safe. The more experienced the seeker, the less easily fooled. Common items will rarely be considered as a place to look for valuables. Books, light bulbs, pens, pencils are less likely to be noticed by an amateur searcher.

Remember to consider all three of these questions when hiding: Who is likely to be looking for your treasure? What type of valuable are you hiding? What is the best hiding method?

Anybody can hide money in a sugar bowl or in a golf bag, or put valuables in a rolled-up sock or under linen in the closet, but how about finding a spot that is less likely to be discovered? After all, the usual reason to hide something is to keep it from being found.

TWO RULES OF HIDING

To use the screening approach, there are two rules to remember:
(1) Any volume is suspect.
(2) Concept/Construction/Context.

Rule (1) means that any item—a wall or article of furniture—that could have hollow space in it could be used as a hiding place. Someone who is searching may know this as well as you do. In the "Purloined Letter," Poe gives an account of an unbelievably thorough search by police—*everything* is suspected and tested! This viewpoint can be used by you to create your own hiding place—or by a burglar to find it!

Rule (2) means that it is not enough to think of a good hiding place. It must be built well-enough to avoid detection, located in a spot consistent with its surroundings, and inconspicuous. Any one of these—concept/construction/context—by itself is not enough; all three must be considered.

Concept

By thinking of an idea for your hiding place instead of simply stashing your valuables the first place you think of, you can break the usual patterns of concealment. Without a consistent pattern, the searcher will be frustrated in trying to locate your valuables. Try to be inconsistent and avoid setting up patterns. If a valuable has several parts or components, they could be located in several places instead of grouped together. Marketing psychologists for supermarkets try to locate separate items of a meal close together in the store to make it easier for the shopper to buy related items. They like to design displays in terms of whole meals, to "tie in" items that would usually be located in different parts of the store.

The field of marketing offers other helpful hints. In a supermarket the items which the management wants to sell most quickly are placed in well-lighted areas and at eye level. This technique can be used in reverse to select a hiding place. Look for a poorly lit area that is well above or below eye level. Consider both day and night lighting. Probably the first place that occurs to you will be around eye level. This is the most natural place to look for something, which is why marketing techniques work—unless we maintain a constant awareness of them; with awareness comes choice.

A habitual pattern of shoppers is buying the first thing in line. The grabber does the same thing. Keeping valuables away from the doors and windows can make it harder for this burglar.

In choosing a hiding place, remember that the first place that occurs to you will probably also occur to someone else, and the easier the access to the hiding place is, the easier it is to find. As an idea for a hiding place romps around your mind, consider how others will use the room. Could a friend accidentally discover your hiding place? Count on inquisitive, energetic, and clumsy friends to jiggle, wiggle, jostle, and fondle every single item in the room, and plan accordingly. If another person can come in and use the room without stumbling across or suspecting your hiding place, then well done!

Construction

Once you become involved with the idea of hiding, one aspect will become very apparent: although the choice of the hiding place is important, it is *vital* to execute it well, and to construct it carefully. A well-done job will require a lot of work, time, skill, and patience. Wandering eyes can easily pick out incongruous details. If the searcher is not looking carefully, they will not be seen. This allows simple hiding places to function satisfactorily with nonburglar guests. A burglar, however, is geared to look for this type of defense. It is not what you do that is important, but the way you do it.

The formula for appropriate construction is
Low Energy = High Risk.

The less energy put into the construction of a hiding place, the higher the risk that it will be found easily.

If using the entry to a secret place scratches or mars any surface of the room or furniture, then it is *no good.* Details are the important part of construction: the entry should not leave a permanent scratch, or break the flow of continuous trim. If one part of a room, such as window frames or door trim, is not painted together with the wall, it will be conspicuous. Painting the frame or trim a different color than the wall, or using varnished wood, would help disguise a hiding place. When repainting, fill cracks between the wall and molding. If you do not, they will be noticeably different. In using wood, use the least visually distinctive wood, which will attract less attention. Keep the basic decor of the room consistent. Consider the effect of usage on the material. Sliding a trapdoor or hidden panel back and forth causes wear marks. If an inexpensive piece of lumber is not kiln-dried, it can warp. Then the secret will no longer be cloaked.

One precaution should be kept in mind: be aware of how items are used, not necessarily the way they *should* be used, but how they really *are* used. For example, do not hollow out structural members, such as the clothes pole in a closet. If too weakened, it could collapse under the weight of your clothes, or if someone tried to do chin-ups on the bar. If your friends use furniture only as intended, then perhaps a chair rung can safely be hollowed out. Otherwise, this is probably not a safe bet.

Context

A brilliantly conceived and beautifully constructed hiding place located in the wrong surroundings will stick out and announce itself to all comers. Put trapdoors and access panels in dark corners, in closets, in out-of-the-way, inconspicuous places. The hardest part of building and having a hiding place is to resist the urge to show it off.

STEPS TO A HIDING PLACE

Now, using the Two Rules, here is a set of questions for you to answer. The answers will help you find an appropriate stash.

1. *What are you hiding?* Consider its size, shape, value. Items that have low market value, such as items of personal sentimental value, do not need a high-energy hiding place. There is little chance of their being stolen.
2. *How often will the hiding place be used?* If frequent access is needed, then it should be easy to use. It is important that frequent use not mar any surfaces.
3. *Who are the items being hidden from?* Your answer here will determine the quality of the construction. If you are hiding something from children, then perhaps simply placing the items well above their eye level will suffice. If, on the other hand, you are expecting the entire Treasury Department to descend on your counterfeiting operation, this would call for a rather more thorough operation.

4. *What type of construction is involved?* An older, re-modeled, wood frame house is easier to modify than a solid stone castle; hidden construction is more appropriate in a house you own than in a summer rental.
5. *What personal skills* (including patience) *and resources* (tools, materials, finance) *are available?* It is foolhardy to begin an elaborate scheme if the finished construction would require more skills and materials than you have. It is better to choose a less elaborate scheme or hire a trusted friend to build it. Maybe a tremendous idea will have to be modified until the necessary tools, money, time, or skills are acquired. This is ok; just decide on a scheme that uses what is available.

USING MISDIRECTION

No less energy is required for this approach, but the emphasis shifts: more concept, less construction, and almost entirely context. Sometimes the item that is the most obvious is the hardest to find. This is the basic point in "The Purloined Letter." The person hiding the valuable letter simply changed the expected pattern. Security-system designers sometimes use an *open-system* approach. Instead of hiding the safe in the back of a store, they mount it by the front window with a light on it. The specific approaches are limited only by the imagination. Using the concept of misdirection is usually more difficult than using a screening technique. It is difficult to remove oneself from the scheme enough to view the results objectively.

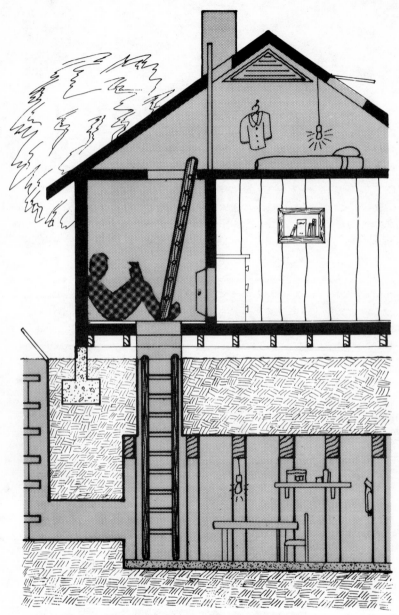

Figure 4.1. The second house within a house.

The Art of Hiding People

To feel daily the presence of a secret room in our home, to
know we have a place to which we can retreat at a moment's
notice and not be found, whether we ever use it or not, can
bring us support and a secret relief, just knowing it is there!
It gives us a solid security, this secret chamber, and helps us
feel more independent in our daily life. Why retreat like this?
Ah, in addition to simply relaxing, sometimes writers and
readers, artists and studiers, thinkers and meditators, need
solitude. The joy of expression often needs to begin from the
inner peace found while alone.

An old social custom in India responds to this need to
be alone in a simple manner: when a large family lives together in a small house, a member can find solitude by step-
ping outside verbal communication while remaining actually
in the house. Once the family accepts the nonverbal request,
they will not talk to nor expect talk from the quiet member.

Since we have no such custom, we need to find visual
privacy, whether for our own retreat or to help someone else
vanish. A political or legal situation sometimes requires complete invisibility for survival. The Christians found this when
they began, the Catholics while reentering England, and the
Jews during World War II.

Existing subterranean chambers offer enough privacy
for group meetings. Caves are often used to hide in. Separated from the house, they are harder for the searchers to find.

A heavily forested area can provide temporary hiding. Massive rocky regions have been used by bandits, both for hiding and for defense. Tree houses have been used for centuries. Some preindustrial societies lived in them.

An underground hideout can be connected to a house or even buried beneath it. Such a room can be useful as a totally undisturbed bedroom, a quiet chamber to meditate or think, an occasional retreat, a place for friends to vanish. If it is connected both to the house and to the outside, it could double as a means to spy on enemy occupants without their knowing. For this purpose, even a space directly under the house would work. An existing basement would rule out an easily concealed subterranean space, however; so a hidden room can be considered at floor level.

The effectiveness of a secret room will depend heavily on the floorplan. In most recent buildings—houses, apartments, offices—floor areas are well-defined and carefully laid out. With this type of floor plan, the existence of a concealed area of any reasonable size will be obvious. Older homes, designed with different criteria, offer an easier situation. Because of the random pattern of the rooms, the floorplan is more difficult to perceive as a whole. Even in these houses, the risk of discovery is higher if the floor area is easily measured in relation to other rooms. Corrie ten Boom's home was perfect in this sense, since two houses had been combined which had floors at different levels! Sherlock Holmes, in "The Adventure of the Norwood Builder," discovers a hidden room at the end of a corridor by comparing measurements between parallel corridors. A partition with a concealed door had been built across the hallway. Small openings under the eaves allowed in light and fresh air.

When designing a hidden room, find a spot that cannot be easily discovered. A closet at the end of a room can be closed up and another closet built in front of it (Figure 4.2). However, if someone suspects that a hidden room exists, one

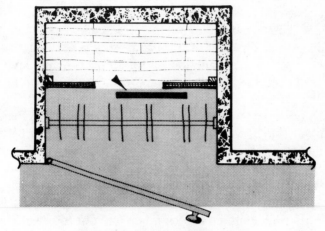

Figure 4.2. Hidden room in a closet.

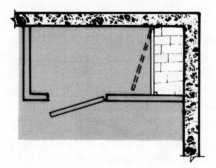

Figure 4.3. Concealed door.

of the first places they will check is in the back of closets; so it is best to have an entrance through the ceiling or the floor.

Once the ground floor has been amply filled with secret chambers, the attic remains to be explored. A garret offers a large space if access and light sources can be sufficiently concealed. When a person is going to be staying in a hidden room for an extended period of time, some source of daylight should be included. Anne Frank longed for all the sun and daylight she could get, long before her two years were up. A false vent pipe or chimney would let in some light and, carefully done, could avoid detection under the closest scrutiny (see Figure 4.4). A skylight would let in a reasonable amount of light but would be easy to spot. Vent pipes are found above kitchens, bathrooms, and furnace rooms. To be least obvious, add the pipes over these areas of the house.

Chimneys will work only in certain areas of the house. To indiscriminately build a chimney on your roof would be a dead giveaway. An older building is easier for this, since in many of them the fireplaces were walled over when gas heating became available. Have you ever wandered around the roof of an older house and tried to discover where all those pipes and chimneys go to inside? Forget it! Without tearing out walls it would be near impossible to know for certain. The only trick to creating a false chimney on an older house is to make the new chimney look as old as the originals. Perhaps one of the originals can be moved, like the common one-piece clay pipes, and reattached at another spot.

Most attics have vent screens to prevent the build-up of hot air during the summer and to prevent condensation. To maintain authenticity, stay within the guidelines of normal vent location. Frequently, more of these are added if the venting is inadequate. Some types of vents can be modified to provide a view. Another approach is to merely place a large vent pipe over an existing small pipe and cut through the roof.

Concealing the access to the attic can be as difficult as cloaking a false door. For example, a small closet could screen

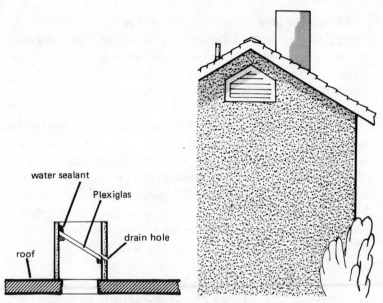

Figure 4.4. *Left:* False attic vent. *Right:* False vent or chimney.

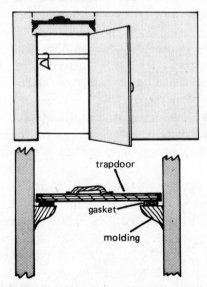

Figure 4.5. Through the closet to the attic. A rubber or cloth gasket blocks the sound of the trapdoor, as well as voices or light from the attic.

a ladder to the attic. Easier to hide and harder to use would be simply a trapdoor in the top of a closet; however, if you substitute a strong pipe for the clothes pole, it could be used to step up into the loft. Another access could be through a trapdoor in the ceiling of a room. If hinged from the top, it would not be visible from below.

The downstairs door must open in a quiet, little-used area. Otherwise, it could not be used for a last-minute escape. The entry door must open in a way that does not disturb the room or leave scratch marks. The people entering must not leave marks on walls, ceilings, or anything else. Such marks allowed Holmes to find the room in "The Adventure of the Golden Pince-nez." Remember, anyone who is specifically looking for a hidden room in your house will observe faulty details that the casual passerby would never notice.

For observing the action in a room from unseen privacy, a two-way mirror, properly placed and constructed, can work visual wonders. With a heavy curtain hung behind the viewer, any accidental flash of light would be veiled from the watched people.

To hide away in a reclusive room, such as the attic, requires special considerations. When unwelcome guests are in the house, sound must be kept to an absolute minimum. A room can be heavily carpeted with lots of sound-absorbing material, to dampen light talk, a gentle sneeze, or an unexpected snore. Telltale light leaks can be prevented by thoroughly sealing any spots where it would show through at night.

The attic could have good ventilation and daylight, provided by vents and/or pipes. Heating could come from an already installed furnace. Artificial lights are easily added. Night flaps over the vents will cut down the risk of lights being seen from outside the house, and well-built sound insulation can allow quiet discussions.

A forced-air heating system with ducts running through the house from the heater unit could have new sections of

ducts added without arousing suspicion. Some of these could
be large enough to get into; all would be big enough for other
valuables. Preferably these sections would not be a functional
part of the heating system! They can appear to join to the
other pipes and yet be blocked off. Standard sheet-metal construction techniques can be used for these warm additions.
The heater unit, a large sheet-metal box, is often found in the
attic and could be added to for a good-size hiding place.

Flat roofs are often cluttered with large pieces of heating and air-conditioning equipment. Some of these could

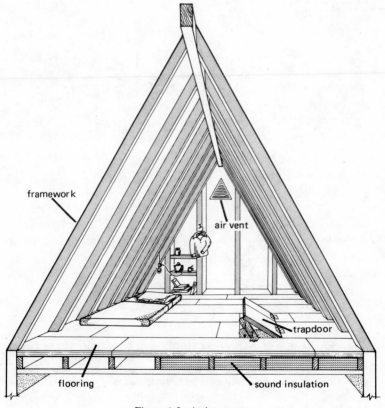

Figure 4.6. Attic retreat.

offer good-size stashes, or more could be added without attracting attention. Parapets around a flat roof could hide a skylight for a hidden room below and also supply alternative access to that space.

An underground room has good-enough sound insulation that a party can carry on even while seekers ramble around at floor level. Light and sufficient air are the biggest challenges for this space. The attic is nearly the opposite: air and light are more accessible, but sound must be kept to a minimum. Floor level is a compromise between these two spaces, yet can offer easier access.

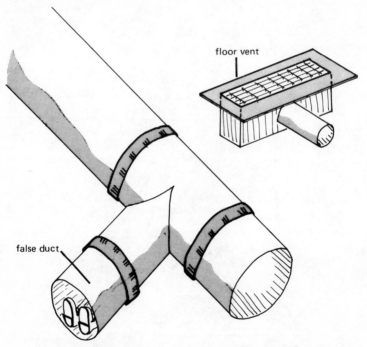

Figure 4.7. Furnace ducts. The pipes used for some furnaces can also be used for unsuspected hiding. A wall vent can be unscrewed and valuables placed within. A floor vent lifts up, and the vent pipe may be large enough for a small person to crawl into. If the furnace is being used, the heat could damage some goods.

Any secret room can be used for valuables instead of, or in addition to, people. Special concealed areas can be built within the chamber. Once a room is built to help people disappear, it becomes a corner they are trapped in. With this in mind, it would be well to have a small retreat extremely well-hidden within the hidden room itself to conceal the hiders in case the room is discovered.

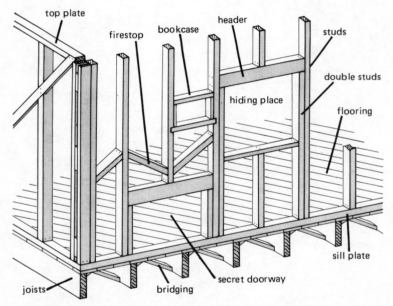

Figure 5.1. Basic framewall construction. This is what you will find once you start to tear a wall apart.

What's in the Wall

The burglar knows! He understands there is a lot of hollow space, and that it can be used for a storehouse of treasure. A builder also knows what's in the wall; so let us end the mystery and peer deep within so that *we* know what is inside . . . and how the wall can be used.

The best way to see how framing, the building's skeleton, is done is to visit a house under construction. Study how the wall is framed, how the diagonal is cut in on the outer wall studs. Observe and practice measuring all parts of the framing that may apply. Measure the distance between studs to practice locating framing members. Notice how firestops, plumbing pipes, and electrical wires fit into the hollow wall. Look at the electric sockets and switches, and how they are attached. To fill in this new knowledge, watch for older houses being torn down or rebuilt, and study the differences from new houses. Carry a tape measure on these trips. In an older house, measure the stud size: it is wider and thicker than what was measured in a new home. The general width of the wall framing and the available space within the wall is about 3½". Older buildings will often have thicker walls. Knowing this basic difference will make construction easier. To test your knowledge, find an inconspicuous place to try a simple construction, such as a shelf in a back room, laundry, or garage. Find the framing, compare the measurements to what they should be, and then you will have a good understanding of how your house is built!

Observe the corners and how the framing leaves little room to use. The construction of a corner connects the ends of two walls together. Every type of corner is filled with structural members. In a plastered house, the corners have a metal strip running from floor to ceiling. There is no hollow space in a corner that is usable for hiding. Stick to the center of the walls themselves. With this knowledge, the abundance of unused, unseen space in a wall can be seen. It can give private storage for well-screened wealth. The full potential of a wall is rarely used!

The basic wall construction in most houses and apartments generally uses this same wood framing in order to meet the requirements of building codes. However, there are endless modifications. Have you ever done remodeling of an older house? If so, then you will know exactly what I mean! Houses vary a lot!

Now we will look at three approaches to using wall space. The first is the basic *cut-in* to the existing framing; the second is to *expand* this space; and the third is to *add on* to the wall.

THE CUT-IN

In this approach you simply cut through the wall's surface and use the space between two adjacent studs. This opens the inner space and exposes a potential treasure chest. The first task is to locate the framing. This can be done with a stud finder (in which an enclosed magnet is attracted to the nails which hold the surface material to the stud), or by tapping with a hammer or finger as if knocking on a door (when the wall is tapped it sounds hollow; the stud sounds deeper and more solid). With an old plaster wall, you may have to measure from the corner and drill spot holes in the area where the stud should be. A simple treasure trove with this approach is a small bookcase (Figure 5.2). A set-in box (Figure 5.3) can be constructed, and fit in snug so that it will not accidentally fall out.

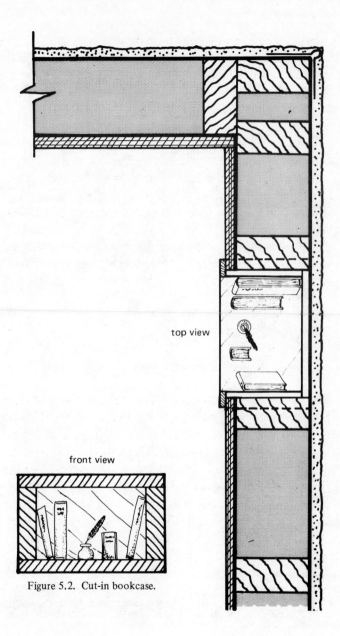

top view

front view

Figure 5.2. Cut-in bookcase.

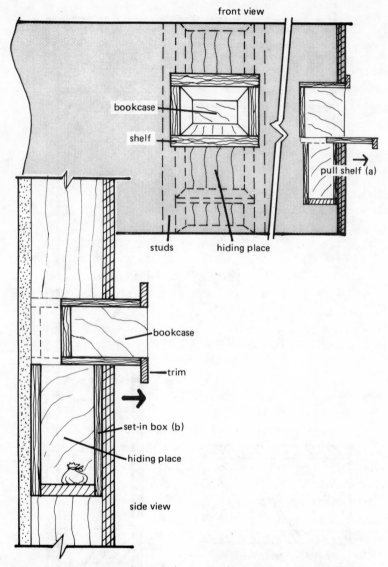

front view

bookcase

shelf

pull shelf (a)

studs

hiding place

bookcase

trim

set-in box (b)

hiding place

side view

Figure 5.3. Using a cut-in bookcase to screen a hiding place. Either the bottom shelf (a) or the entire box (b) can be pulled straight out to reveal the hiding place beneath.

EXPANSION

Expanding the space, extending beyond the limits of the studs, is a larger, more complicated job, and requires special construction, but results in a bigger space. The basic premise here is that the wall will be partially dismantled. Just as with a window, a *header* must absorb the building weight that the removed framing had supported. Before a large section of wall is removed or the framing modified, find out if it is a *bearing wall:* does the wall hold the roof up? Does it bear the weight of the building? If so, a *nonbearing* wall or partition is much easier and safer.

The first step toward modifying a wall is to take apart the surface material around the area where the finished hole will be, so that you can see how the wall is constructed. Once the wall construction is understood, modification becomes a straightforward task. Expanding requires framing knowledge and special construction; whereas a cut-in adapts to the way the wall is already constructed, and does not require as much knowledge of carpentry.

ADDING ON

To *add on* a deeper space or a new wall in front of an existing wall is another possibility. To hide a wall safe or a deep shelf behind a painting or tapestry, the wall must be deeper. A room behind the wall could be used to extend the space deeper than wall thickness; but, except in an ideal situation, the addition would then glare out in that other room. This strategy will work out better if the wall is backed by a closet, to which other hiding places can also be added, as we will see. In the right situation, a second wall could be added in front of the original wall. In a modern home, such a wall must be kept fairly thin, or it will be obvious to passersby.

By making the space within a wall deeper than the standard
3½" and working out a wall's worth of secret doors, you could
keep a vast collection of anything hidden in it. If anyone
stops by and asks why the second wall is being built, tell
them it is for sound insulation; the double wall is a standard
to cut down on noise between rooms. (Maybe there already
is a double wall in your home. Take a look.) Doorways into
the wall can be provided by covering the wall with plywood
paneling and using concealed hinges. And if the second wall
is built a little further away from the first wall, the resulting
space would be a completely hidden room, an ideal place to
stash a stereo and a television: "out of sight, out of mind"—
and hopefully out of the burglar's hands!

Keep two things in mind. First, do not start work on a
wall until any possible wires and pipes in the wall are located.
You could quickly be in serious trouble if you were to drill
or saw through pipes and wires which are hidden to protect
them from unnecessary damage. Cautiously remove a small
piece of wall in one place (Figure 5.4), survey the space within, think of what you saw in the house under construction,
and then decide the best approach for this particular situation.
Second, be sure to replace any firestops which are removed.
When remodeling is done and these are not replaced, a chimney is created inside the wall which can funnel fire through
to another floor.

Either screening or misdirecting can be used to conceal
the access door. Anything hidden in the wall is screened from
view. The access panel or door can be concealed by a clever
misdirecting of the searcher's attention.

Many wondrous possibilities can be exploited if you ac-
quire some skills in carpentry and building. Window sills can
be used, if they are wood sills and are specially altered into
hiding places during construction or remodeling. Removing
trim or molding along the floor or ceiling can reveal hollow
places. People who refinish old moldings often find money
hidden behind or even inside them!

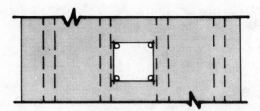

Figure 5.4. To gain access into the wall, drill four holes between the studs.

In or behind light switches or wall plugs, a few small items can be stashed. The inside of a base plate of an overhead light can be filled (with nonconducting treasures!). With any electrical fixtures, use caution. Before delving into these areas, switch off the current. An electrical stash spot provides a greater security against incautious searchers!

The bathroom presents possibilities: perhaps a hamper for dirty clothes will be overlooked by searchers. Medicine cabinets can have a complete shelf that slides aside into the

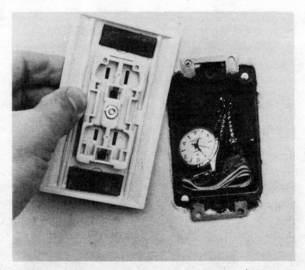

Figure 5.5. Electric plug: *false* outlet box, with no wires attached. The wall plate is held on with magnetic tape (see Appendix A).

Figure 5.6. Homemade outlet box. The plate locks with a tang attached to the center screw.

Figure 5.7. Homemade with different outlet box.

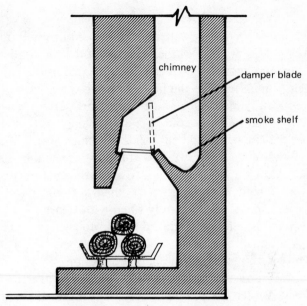

Figure 5.8. Chimney construction.

wall. The entire cabinet could lift out or be secretly hinged
to swing out. The toilet tank can be used, although it is a
high-risk place. The float can be carefully separated and resoldered or glued. Small or lightweight treasures can be concealed here for a long time. The modified float is low-risk, *if*
it is reattached well enough to look like the original. Have
you ever noticed the thickness of the wall behind the toilet?
It is thicker than the standard wall, to carry the pipes, drains,
and vents. This might be a good place for a magazine rack
or . . .

The old trick with a loose brick will only work in a wall
or fireplace that has a lot of loose mortar. Current brick work
is too well-done to allow a loose brick to go unnoticed. Perhaps the wood door next to the fireplace can provide a place
to hide an access panel. Fireplaces are built in many ways. If
a smoke shelf does exist, with access around the damper blade,
it can be a fairly safe place to store nonburnable items.

The space under stairs can offer a wide variety of possible stashes. People or valuable equipment or small items are easily hidden. As long as the stairs are still structurally solid, anything will work. They can be rebuilt underneath and hinged to raise up, like the lid of a storage chest. Given adequate padding, people can hide for a short period. The wooden side of the stairway could lift off, or hinge out. Either the run or the rise of a step could slide out sideways.

Window seats are often used for storage of pillows or quilts. Also, they often open into an unfinished portion of the wall, which, depending on its construction, can offer a concealed space to be securely filled with treasures.

A wall shelf can be hinged on top to swing into a concealed room and latch on the bottom for daily use. It could also be on runners and slide in one direction.

The whole of any house offers a wonderful array of safe hollows. We have explored underground, floor-level, attic, and wall spaces. Now let us consider some additional ideas and possibilities.

UNDER THE FLOOR

Most modern floor construction uses tongue-and-groove boards (Figure 5.9). It is very difficult to pry such boards up from the floor without tearing them, but once they are up, they offer distinct advantages for construction of a trapdoor. Often the easiest way to get the boards up is to begin by sawing off a tongue while the boards are still in place, by careful use of a very thin-bladed saw. The boards can then be pried up without danger of damage.

Bracing is nailed across the bottom of the boards to create the trapdoor, and, if necessary, the edge from which the tongue has been removed can be trimmed down slightly to prevent sticking (Figure 5.10). When the resulting door is in place, it will be virtually undetectable (Figure 5.11). Similar construction can also, of course, be used with square-edge

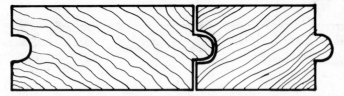
Figure 5.9. Tongue-and-groove floorboards.

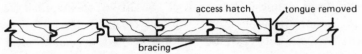
Figure 5.10. Tongue-and-groove trapdoor.

Figure 5.11. Demonstration of a trapdoor.

floorboards (Figure 5.12); here a lip must be created to support the door.

Consider the walls in modern apartments: where would you hide something here? There is no molding, just a single material with no seams. Consider scale: the sizes we are accustomed to seeing vary from very large to almost microscopic. The usual eye-size scale of concealment would not work in this type of wall by itself, but larger or smaller might, or something could be added for misdirecting or for screening (such as a painting or molding which is not painted the same color as the wall). A remodeled house and especially older buildings will already have irregular details which can create possible hiding places. Modern construction of many apart-

Figure 5.12. Trapdoor made in square-edge flooring.

ments conceals all the building structure, vents, and wires. Often these apartments have gypsum wallboard on both the walls and ceilings. The consistent quality of this work leaves little room for hidden nooks. However, as Figure 5.14 shows, even here, where it would not be expected, we can create a hiding place.

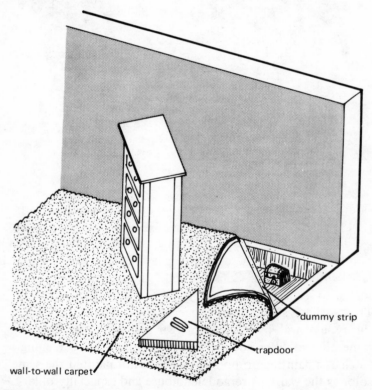

Figure 5.13. Fold back the edge of the carpet, make a trapdoor, and you have a cache hidden beneath the floor.

INSIDE THE DOOR

One of the most common doors in use today is the hollow-core door, which has a frame of wood and is filled with insulation and structural baffles. Such a door can become a hider's delight!

A set of minor hiding places for semipermanent storage can be created by removing the latchplate (Figure 5.14) or

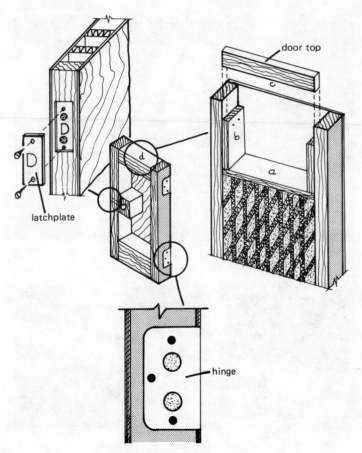

Figure 5.14. Hollow-core door.

the hinges (Figures 5.14 and 5.15), and drilling holes in the areas covered by the metal surfaces. However, the most versatile hiding place is in the top of the door.

To remove the top piece of a door (piece *d* in Figure 5.15), trim around it with a saber saw or tap it out with a screwdriver. Remove the wood block carefully to avoid ripping the doorskin plywood on the door. The bracing inside is a light material like cardboard (Figure 5.16), and can be

Figure 5.15. Usable space under hinges.

Figure 5.16. Construction of a hiding place in a hollow-core door.

easily removed. Now, referring to Figure 5.14, nail the bottom piece (*a*) to the side supports (*b*); drop it down into the door, and nail the side pieces to the door from the inside. Do not make this hole too deep, for then small articles could not be reached. The door would have to be removed and turned upside down to get them out.

The critical part is the top piece (*d*). A small strip must be glued inside the door top on each side (*c*). If not, the doorskin will warp out. Top piece (*d*) will nestle in between the two supports. The finish is not too important with this hiding place, since not many burglars are taller than doors. Just make sure that the top piece does not rattle!

Finally, we can note that many doorknobs unscrew with a small set screw, or unclip from the shaft, and are hollow (Figure 5.17). However, the knob is an easy place to get into, and many searchers know about them and often check them; so it is best to not use them for most valuables.

Figure 5.17. Hollow doorknob.

BETWEEN THE CLOSETS

When two adjoining rooms have closets side-by-side, a hidden compartment can be constructed between them if the conditions and construction are just right (Figure 5.18, *left*). Just as with the false-bottom drawer, if too much space is used, it will be easy to spot. In contrast, in the situation in Figure 5.18, *right,* where the full outside dimensions of the closet are easily measured, a hidden compartment would be difficult to conceal.

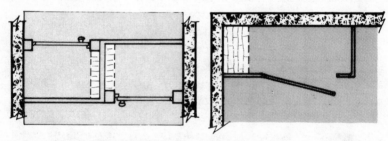

Figure 5.18. *Left:* Concealed space between two closets. *Right:* A concealed space in this closet would be obvious to anyone looking for it.

Another type of storage area that can be used for concealment is the pegboard. Tools are often hung on pegboards for easy access. The board can also cover a hidden toolrack (Figure 5.19); if the boards are set against the wall, rather than within it, a reasonable space is provided. Chamfer the edges carefully (Figure 5.20), so that constant use will not make wear marks, and do not open with oily fingers! Use Soss hinges or recessed piano hinges, so that the door will not show. A simple nail-lock will suffice for security (Figure 5.21): in the metal bracket, one nail is real; the other is in a drilled hole, and can be lifted out to gain access to the secret tools. Another possibility is to hinge the entire board on the top, and prop it up when open (Figure 5.22). This arrangement would be less suspected and is more difficult to use.

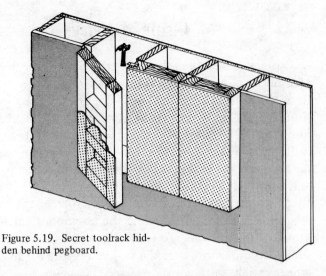

Figure 5.19. Secret toolrack hidden behind pegboard.

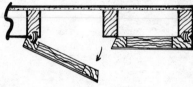

Figure 5.20. Notice hidden hinges and chamfered edges.

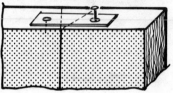

Figure 5.21. Metal bracket serves as disguised lock.

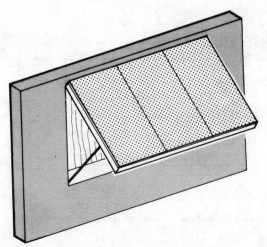

Figure 5.22. Pegboard hinged at top.

INSIDE THE PIPES

Electric metallic tubing, or conduit pipes, can be situated between wall studs, on the ceiling, in the attic, under the floor, or anywhere. If the house does not use conduit, one short length can be explained as remodeling! The trick shown in Figure 5.23 is simple: the end sections are attached to the wall, but the middle section is not. Use the type of pipe connector shown in Figure 5.24. It has a screw close to each end and a projecting band in the center. Cut the pipe sections so that they penetrate the connectors no further than the screws (Figure 5.23a), which will hold the assembly tight when it is mounted on the wall. To remove the pipe, loosen the screws, slide the connectors over the middle (Figure 5.23b), and it will ease right out!

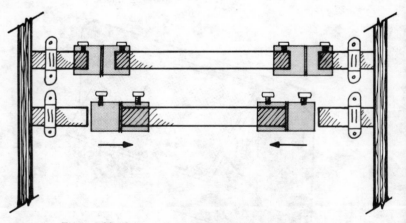

Figure 5.23. False conduit: (a) mounted; (b) ready to remove.

Figure 5.24. Pipe connector.

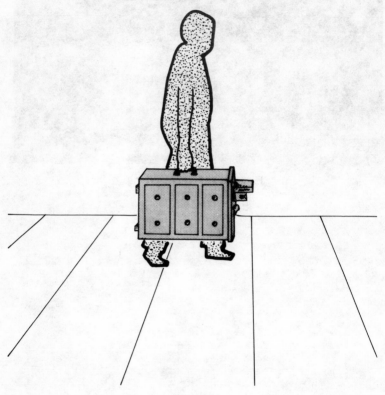

Figure 6.1

Moveable Hidlings

Since many people in our society move frequently, and since landlords do not take too kindly to having their property modified in any way, let us consider the advantages of building hiding places into personal property, such as furniture, books, or lamps, which can be carried along when one moves,

Even though all the ways to stash valuables may be considered, only *one* place is needed, if it is well-conceived and constructed, and located in an appropriate spot. The variations you develop will take the cache beyond anyone else's ideas and give it enough originality to throw a searcher off.

Cash and documents are often hidden in a rolled-up window shade. The FBI has found bank robber's loot in this place. A small hole can be drilled in the end of the shade roller. The weights in the bottom of curtains are not always lead! This can be a tremendous place to conceal an old necklace or anything that is flexible, long, and heavy. Look around the rest of the living room, the room most frequently used by guests. Any piano has a partially hollow back. An upright piano is best, since it is less likely to be opened. And just think: you can sit upon the piano bench with secret compartments and hear the music bless the treasures near the strings with its rich tones!

In this chapter the possibilities in a chest of drawers will be explored. At the end of World War II, a soldier and his friend decided to do some target practice. After much unsuccessful looking for a target pistol, they heard the black market was good for guns. They wandered about the streets asking vendors. Finally one heard their questions and said, "Guns? Come with me." They followed him through streets

61

and alleys, into the darkest part of town, and finally up a stairway. When the door was opened, they were escorted into an incredibly elegant room, filled with ornate furnishings. When they were seated, their host went to a chest of drawers and started pulling out guns from every place—except the drawers! They watched him do this, but could still not figure out where he got all the guns, enough to fill a whole table in front of them!

In old Japan a merchant's chest was used to store business papers, pens, and ink. This chest is a *cho dansu,* and often secrets, money, or jewels were hidden amongst its graceful lines.

Throughout history, portable possessions have been a favorite place for concealing tempting treasures. The screening approach makes anything with volume suspect; imaginative misdirecting can make use of any object we carry about with us. Remember to consider who the searcher may be; a robber and a custom agent have similar skills but different purposes. They enjoy your skill in hiding as much as you do!

THE HIDING CHEST

The simple dresser shown in Figure 6.3 has at least 12 hiding places! As numbered in Figure 6.4, they are:

- (1) hinged top;
- (2) hinged back;
- (3–6) false-bottom drawers;
- (7–9) space between drawers;
- (11–12) spaces on the chest sides.

These ideas cover only the already existing spaces. Hollow knobs could be added to the drawers; the top or corner braces could be hollowed out; the drawers could all be fake, leaving the whole chest hollow; and so on.

Figure 6.2. A *cho dansu.*

Figure 6.3. An ordinary-looking chest of drawers.

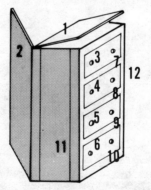

Figure 6.4. The same chest of drawers has 12 hiding places.

The Hinged Top

The hinged dresser top (Figure 6.5) is less likely to be discovered than a false-bottom drawer; it also takes more effort to construct. Use Soss hinges (Figure 6.6), which are not visible from outside, but must be mounted very carefully. The hidden shelf is harder to detect if it is placed a finger length away from the front of the chest, to avoid curious fingers. The top is locked by sliding bolts, reached from beneath by opening the top drawer; they are easy to use and can have a rattle-free snug fit.

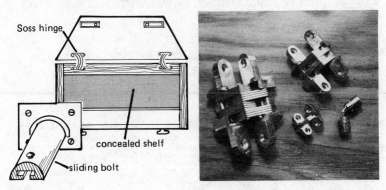

Soss hinge

concealed shelf

sliding bolt

Figure 6.5. *Left:* The hinged top. *Right:* Soss hinges are available in many sizes at hardware stores.

Figure 6.6. The hinged-top chest in use.

False-bottom Drawers

In the false-bottom drawer, the bottom slides out to give access to the hiding place (Figure 6.7). We will deal with two types of false-bottom drawer: Type A requires no tools; Type B requires several tools, but is less likely to be detected.

The first step for both A and B is to remove the bottom from the drawer. The back end of the bottom is nailed or stapled to the back piece of the drawer. Pull these nails or staples out carefully, so that scratches will not give you away; when the false bottom is complete, it must look *exactly* the same as it did before construction was started, or else it will not be a secret. One way to get the nails or staples out without leaving pry marks is to hold a piece of wood inside the drawer against the back piece and pound gently with a hammer from the inside (Figure 6.8). This will loosen the fasteners, and they can be removed. Since the bottom is probably held in with a dado cut (a groove cut in the sides of the drawer), hammering from inside can loosen the nails. To remove them, put a thin piece of wood under the hammer's claws before pulling the fasteners out. This prevents any impression on the wood.

Once the bottom of the drawer is removed, decide on either Type A or Type B. In choosing the material for the false bottom, try to find some that is identical to the original bottom. If you cannot, use the bottom from another drawer. If you find the identical material in a lumber yard, they will cut it to size; so a saw will not be needed.

To do drawer A, gather small pieces of wood to set the false bottom on. These do not need to go the full length of the drawer, but the bottom will be more solid if they do. Glue these to the false bottom (Figure 6.9), and press with a lot of weight to make a good bond. A set of encyclopedias, a spare tire, anything to keep it pressed while it dries. When it is dry, it can be either glued into the drawer or attached more securely by nailing. Use short nails, so that they will

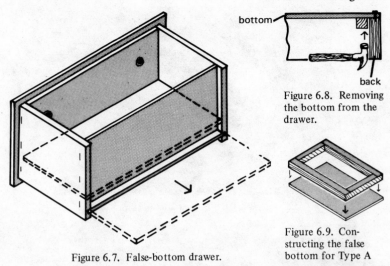

Figure 6.8. Removing the bottom from the drawer.

Figure 6.9. Constructing the false bottom for Type A

Figure 6.7. False-bottom drawer.

not show from the outside. Slip the original bottom back in and hammer the fasteners in place. With either type, the original fasteners for the bottom can be cut shorter. At the right length, they will stay in the holes, but will be easy to remove with finger pressure; so the bottom will look original, yet access will be easy.

The least detectable is Type B, in which the construction of the original drawer is copied; so the modifications will be difficult to spot. With the bottom removed, carefully dismantle the whole drawer. Dado an appropriate size groove around the inside; copy the original dado, and include a dado in the back-piece of the drawer. Slip in the false bottom, and nail the drawer back together. Put the original bottom back in, and secure your treasures. Be sure to wrap anything hidden in the new compartment with ample soft cloth, so that it will not rattle around.

The finished false bottom is shown in Figure 6.10. Remember, the shallower the depth, the less obvious the false bottom will be. For comparison, a Type A drawer is shown in Figure 6.11, and a Type B drawer in Figure 6.12.

Figure 6.10. Finished false bottom.

Figure 6.11. Type A drawer.

Figure 6.12. Type B drawer.

The Hinged Back

As can be seen in Figure 6.13, a lot of space exists between the drawers, and it can be used in many ways. There is also space under the bottom. The hinged back could open onto secret drawers between the other drawers which open from the front. It could also be used to store large, flat goods between the shelves and the back.

To hinge the back, Soss or piano hinges can be used along the vertical edge. If the back is too thin to carry a Soss hinge, a strip of wood can be attached, as was done with the hinged top. A top latch can be included under a hinged top, or a well-concealed release lever could be included in a dresser with the right sort of trim.

Figure 6.13. Rear view of the chest of drawers.

THE FAKE BOOK

More secrets can be hidden in books than were ever printed in them. Here are instructions on how to construct a fake book from scratch. The over-all construction is shown in Figure 6.14, *left,* the finished product in Figure 6.14, *right.*

(1) Choose an old paperback book that is as large and thick as you want the finished book to be. The width and length determine the size of the enclosed space. If you choose a book that is somewhat thicker than the finished product will be, you can save the extra pages in case some pages tear later.

(2) Cut a block of pages out of the center of the old book. Use a linoleum cutter, cutting a few pages at a time, and use a straight edge to keep the pages down and to make a straight cut. Fold the cut pages back as you go to expose

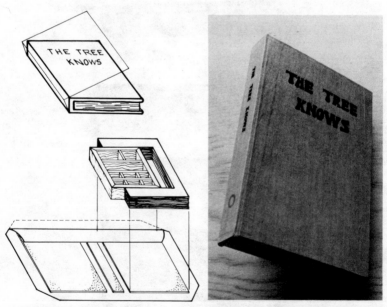

Figure 6.14: *Left:* Construction of a fake book. *Right:* And what does the tree know?

the uncut pages. By doing so, you will not need to make a
deep cut, and will be able to keep the cut straight.

(3) Design and build a box or compartments to fit inside the pages. The spaces should be planned for the size of
the goods to be hidden.

(4) Choose the boards for the cover. Poster board gives
good thickness and flexibility. Cut front and back boards with
an eighth-inch border, so it will appear to be a real book when
finished. Assemble the boards, the pages, and the box; then
measure the thickness of all these pieces assembled together.

(5) Choose the material to bind the book with. Look
at hardbound books, and notice what their covers are made
of. Cut the material as shown in Figure 6.16.

(6) You can make traditional binding glue by adding
cold water to a small amount of whole wheat flour; mix (preferably in a blender) to remove all the lumps. As it becomes
the thickness of thin cream, put it in a pan, and add twice
its volume of boiling water. Stir until it is thick, and boil for
two minutes. If it is too thick when cool, it can be thinned
with cold water. Use a paint or basting brush to apply.

(7) It is best to glue the book together in three separate
steps—at least the first time you try this.

First, brush glue over the entire inside of the cover material, carefully position the boards, and fold the material
over them. This is the most important part, for when it is well
done, the result will look like a real book! When it is all glued
and smoothed out flat, put a piece of plastic food wrap (or
other non-stick material) over the entire inside. Before the
glue begins to set, put in the pages and the box, position them
exactly, and carefully fold the cover and plastic around them.
Put a lot of weight on top, and let the glue set overnight until
dry.

Second, apply glue on the material for the inside of the
cover, carefully set it into the cover, and repeat the drying
procedure, using the plastic again.

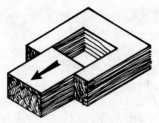

Figure 6.15. Hollowing out a paper-back.

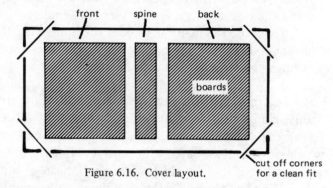

Figure 6.16. Cover layout.

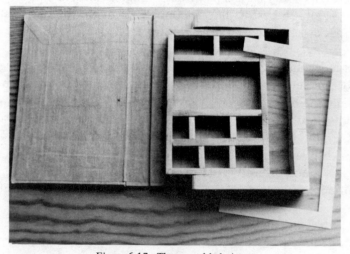

Figure 6.17. The assembled pieces.

Third, brush glue on the *inside* of the old book pages. This holds the pages together, and the glue will not show on the outside. Wiggle the pages to let the glue seep in between pages, then glue the bottom of the pages and set into position on the cover. Glue the bottom of the box, and put it in place. Repeat the drying procedure, and your *new* book will be finished, and will look like a real book!

The Hollow Book

When deciding on a book to hollow out, try to pick a title that is not likely to be casually taken off the shelf by a browsing friend. This decision can be difficult, because it must take into account what kinds of books are already on the shelf, who the friends are, and what interests they have. Also, the book must blend in inconspicuously. A *Reader's Digest* book will be prominent and highly suspect in a library that consists mainly of leftist literature; whereas in a comfortable middle-class home, it may sit undisturbed by any visitors. Keep in mind the unspoken consequences a hiding place can bear for its user; the responsibilities a hollow book demands can be far-reaching.

As you ponder the first, ghastly cut to an innocent book, consider tailoring the whole to fit the object being hidden (as in Figure 6.19), to avoid much needless rattle. Hardbound books are usually used for hollowing out, and some methods will also work with paperbacks. Here are some methods to enrich your book case.

To cut a neat hole, use a sharp knife. Cut only a few pages at a time, since some types of paper will bunch up in knots ahead of the knife blade and will rip. To make neat corners, cut *away* from the corners, not into them (Figure 6.20). This also prevents the paper knots from forming. Keep the knife perpendicular to the page while cutting, or the hole will not be straight. A thin cutting board, such as tag board,

Figure 6.18. A hollow book.

Figure 6.19. Hole tailored to the object.

Figure 6.20. Cut *away* from the corners.

placed under every few pages as you cut them will help achieve a neat hollow.

If a hole is merely cut through the required number of pages, and they are left to flop loosely around, the valuable item is not as secure as if the pages are glued together. A simple and effective way to glue them is to brush binding glue on the inside of the pages. That is, glue the pages from the inside of the hole. This seals the cavity yet leaves the outside of the pages free and normal-looking. To do a fancier job and to further protect the encased treasure, cloth can be glued into the hole. Do not use white glue; it is not flexible when dry, and will crack with use.

Alternatively, with a paperback (as in Figure 6.19), you can pour a lot of glue into the hole, and brush it onto the pages in the hole. Flip the pages about to let the glue seep between them. Put a non-stick sheet, such as aluminum foil or plastic wrap, over the first page with a hole in it; otherwise, the hole will be hidden even from you! Again, stack weight on the book until it is dry.

A final variation is the spine cut (Figure 6.21). Here are the instructions:

(1) Cut through the edge of the spine on the *back* of the book.
(2) Decide the hole size, and cut through the book to the desired depth.
(3) Cut the slot through the spine, and pull the cut section out.
(4) Glue the pages together *inside* the hole. Let dry.

Figure 6.21. The spine-cut hollow book.

THE HOLLOW LIGHT BULB

Here is how you can make a hiding space in an ordinary light bulb.

(1) Using wire cutters, clip off the metal disk on the bottom (see Figure 6.22).

(2) Chip away the glass under the disk—*carefully*—with a small hammer, or wedge a screwdriver in the hole and twist.

(3) When the glass is all broken out of the base, break the wire holding the filament, and either pull it out with small pliers or shake it out.

(4) The bulb itself adheres to the base. Now, carefully reach in with a screwdriver or small pliers, and clean the ragged edge of the remaining glass.

(5) Wash out the bulb to insure that all the small glass splinters have been removed.

(6) Fill with goodies and put in an inconspicuous lamp. Colored bulbs are best; the contents do not show as easily.

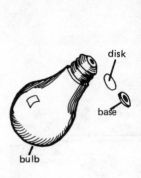

Figure 6.22. *Left:* Removing the bottom disk from a light bulb. *Right:* The hollow bulb: before and after.

THE FALSE-TOP TABLE

In Figure 6.23, the chess board itself can simply lift out to reveal a hidden compartment. The compartment should not be so deep that its existence is obvious. A solid top with side entry into the compartment would be more challenging to construct and easier to use. A sliding release (Figure 6.24) would secure the chess board, like a Chinese puzzle, and make it easily accessible.

THE MAGICIAN'S BLACK BOX

When you look into the empty bottom compartment of the magic box, the mirror creates the illusion that you are seeing the whole volume of the box, instead of just half. The illusionist opens the bottom compartment, puts his hand in to demonstrate that the box is empty, and misdirects the attention of the audience while he turns the box. He then reaches in and pulls out the scarves or other props from the compartment at the back of the mirror. By having only one

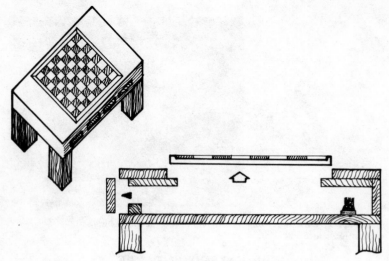

Figure 6.23. The false-top table.

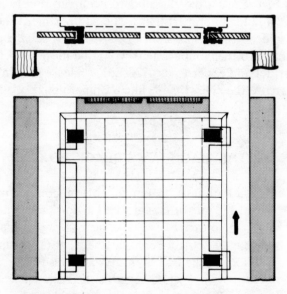

Figure 6.24. False top is released when strips are slid sideways.

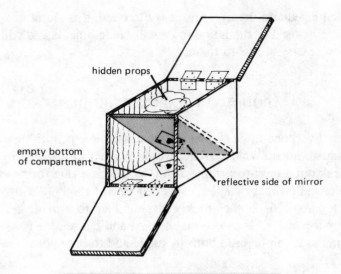

hidden props

empty bottom
of compartment

reflective side of mirror

Figure 6.25. The magician's black box (display
courtesy of Richard Lloyd).

side hinged and the other not easy to open, this secret box could be used in the home to casually hide objects and still provide easy access to them.

AROUND AND ABOUT THE DESK

Everyone has a stapler on the desk; there is nothing un-usual about it. What searcher would suspect or bother to check out a desk-top stapler? Ah, so here is a clue for the hider: an ordinary stapler, especially one of the kind shown in Figure 6.26, can be quickly disassembled to provide a desk-top cache. It can be taken apart and reassembled any-time; so it can be used both to staple and to hide your trea-sures!

A desk that is fancy enough to have a secret compart-ment (Figure 6.27) is rather hard to come by, but most

Figure 6.26. The hollow stapler.

Figure 6.27. Secret compartment in desk (display courtesy of Wells Hoeltje).

people keep a few silly-looking items on their desks, and these can screen a cache (Figure 6.28, *upper left*). The telephone is a natural item to have on a desk; did you know that the handpiece is hollow? It has to be large enough to be comfortable to hold; yet it carries nothing but one thin wire (Figure 6.28, *upper right*). A thief would never bother with the snack you've left sitting on the back of your desk (Figure 28, *lower left*). Even a metal desk offers its own advantages; there are magnetic devices that can be slipped onto the undersurfaces or backs of drawers (Figure 28, *lower right*).

Figure 6.28. *Upper left:* Disguising a cache as a memento. *Upper right:* The hollow handpiece of the telephone. *Lower left:* Hollow can and bottle (see Appendix A). *Lower right:* A magnetic keyholder and a Magna-Stash (see Appendix A).

Finally, as an example of how a small household item can function as a stash, consider the antique candleholder in Figure 6.29.

Figure 6.29. A concealed compartment in an antique candleholder.

Hiding Places in the Home

These places are known both to burglars and to the police. Use imaginative misdirecting in using them. This list can give you an insight into the mind of both the searcher *and* the hider.

Under or in the mailbox
Inside candlestick holders

In flower pots and window boxes

Hiding Places in the Home (Cont.)

Inside hollow doors (removable tops)

Inside door chimes and door bell

Behind plumbing-inspection doors

In doorknobs

In dog collars

Hanging out windows

Rolled up in window shades

On the window ledge next door

On top of windows, door sills, moldings

In fire and water hoses

In cellar beams

Taped to movable clothesline

Behind exterior brick near window

In fuse box

In fire-alarm bell

In dog houses

In rain gutters and drain spouts

Inside abandoned plumbing

Inside attic insulation

In furnace

In hollowed-out tree

In fuel of oil heaters

Under lip ring of plastic trash cans

In conduit from fuse box

Under tile steps of back yard

Under fence post tops

Inside rabbit hutch

In pay-telephone coin return

In clothesline pipe

Inside garbage disposal

In electric baseboard heaters

Inside string mop

In refrigerator: inside fruit containers, inside mayonnaise, under food, taped under door, inside meat compartment

Under ironing board cover

In bottom of dog food bag

In bottom half of double boiler

In ironing-board legs

In eggs

On toaster tray

Inside plastic rolling pin

Inside clock

In hot-air ducts

In stove pipes

In garbage bags

In Bromo Seltzer bottle

In cookies and candy bars

In baked bread, cookies, brownies.

Built inside room dividers

Behind kick plates of sink cabinets

In stove insulation, exhausts, and drip pans

In tea bags

In acoustical-tile ceilings

Inside tinfoil tube

Inside paper-towel tube

In salt and pepper shakers

In waxed paper dispensers

In spice jars

In hollowed fruits and vegetables

In chandelier

In agitator of washer

In venetian blinds

In fluorescent light tubes

Hiding Places in the Home (Cont.)

In telephone base and handle

In wall and ceiling light fixtures

In removable air-conditioning registers

In range hood and filter

Inside deep-well fryers

Behind base boards

In flashlights

In douche bags

Within sanitary napkins and in box

In razor-blade dispenser

In prescription bottles

In hollowed-out flashlight batteries

In talcum and cold-cream containers

In electric-toothbrush holder

In toothpaste tubes

In clothes hamper

Hung behind curtains

Inside false ceilings and chimneys

In all kitchen canisters and containers

Inside knife handles

Behind wall phones

In sink traps

In base of lamp

Under washbowl, sink, or tub

In pet box

Inside light switches

Inside hollow curtain rods, shower curtain rods, and closet rods

Inside false bottom on radiator covers

Inside toilet tanks

Inside toilet-bowl float

Taped to top of toilet bowl

In false aerosol cans

In bandaids and bandaid boxes

In stick-deodorant containers

In cold-cream and vaseline jars

In hollow soap bars

Under panel of parquet floors

Inside toilet-paper roll

In clothespin bag

Inside hollow handle of toilet-bowl brush

In after-shave, cologne, or cosmetic bottles

Behind and inside medicine cabinets

In shaving-brush handle

In hair dryer

In shower-nozzle head

In razor-blade disposal

In leg of old-style bath tub

In clothing in closet: waistbands, pens, sleeves, hatbands, shoes, gloves

Behind picture frames, posters, and mirrors

In mattresses

Under carpets

Inside and under wigs

Behind walls

In bed posts

In furniture upholstery

In golf bags

In toys, stuffed animals and games

In child's bank

In electrical sockets

Taped in dresser and behind drawers

In concealed magnetic boxes

Hiding Places in the Home (Cont.)

In zippered cushions and pillows

Inside pipe-rack stand

In false-bottom baby carriages and cribs

In footlockers

In hem of drapes and curtains

Hid in mattress frame or box-springs

In pillow cases

In seams of field cots and hollow cap of cot legs

Inside hassock

In hidden drawers in tables

Inside letters

In dolls

In art kits

In Holy Bible (hollow cover)

In other books (hollowed pages)

In jewelry box

Mixed with tobacco

Taped to hat or shoe boxes

Under number plate of telephone

Inside tube and barrel of air rifle

In bird cage

In typewriters and covers

In chess pieces and board

In hollow cane

In chimney clean out

In drops on graph paper

In base of rabbit antenna

Inside TV set

Inside TV antenna

Inside altered picture tube or other components

In hollowed-out pad of paper

In light housing

In surfboards, skis, and other sports equipment

Inside Christmas-tree decorations

Inside handle of Kirby vacuum cleaners

Inside and behind vacuum-cleaner bags

In tool box

In shoe-polish container and equipment

In 35-mm film cans

Inside cameras

In record albums

In fish tanks

Inside patch trap of antique rifle

Inside rifle cartridges and shotgun shells

In rifle-barrel buttplate

Inside handle of carpenter's toolbox

Inside ceramic and clay figurines

Inside rolled-up newspaper

Inside trophies

In floor drain

In test tubes

Inside crucifix

In sealed and opened cigarette packages

Inside stairway posts

Inside transistor radio

Inside speakers

Inside other stereo components

In magazines and books

In musical instruments and cases

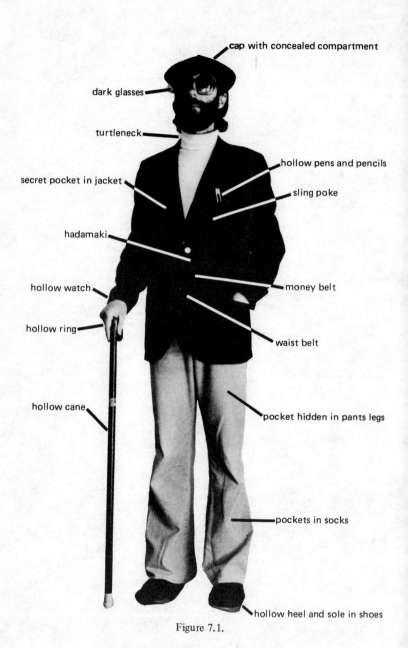

cap with concealed compartment

dark glasses

turtleneck

hollow pens and pencils

sling poke

secret pocket in jacket

hadamaki

money belt

hollow watch

hollow ring

waist belt

hollow cane

pocket hidden in pants legs

pockets in socks

hollow heel and sole in shoes

Figure 7.1.

Body Hide

The possibilities for hiding places while one is traveling are unlimited. A successful hiding place counts not just on screening the looker's vision, but also on making use of the particular situation the traveler will be in, on a train, in a hotel, etc. The best hiding place is in the item that is in normal, daily use, since it will be easily overlooked. To break through the patterns that thieves expect and conceal valuables in novel ways can almost guarantee you a journey that is safe from loss.

Thieves know how people from a particular culture will hide their money, passport, jewelry, and other valuables when traveling. Pickpockets watch a male victim to see which pocket he touches while walking. Then they know which pocket carries the wallet. The approach used to misdirect the house burglar must be used here. The first way to hide that the traveler thinks of is probably a method heard from friends, or seen in movies or books. Thieves have also heard them. To break the usual patterns of hiding is challenging, since it involves misdirecting a person who will be dealt with face-to-face. Finding a new pattern can take the hider into new, imaginative methods and into ones used by other cultures. Long ago, before wood doors were in use in the Near East, people stored their wealth in the jewelry they wore. This was the safest way to protect one's wealth.

As Figure 7.1 shows, many stashes can be found on and about the clothing. In shoes, a hollow heel (Figure 7.2) is an old and well-used screen. If the sole is thick enough, the inner liner can be lifted out, a hollow spot carved in, and the liner placed back on top. Socks can be a temporary stash for money or other flat objects. The pants can have secret pockets sewn inside. Money belts (Figure 7.3) are a useful way to carry cash and other small items; they may never be suspected, because they *are* so old and frequently used. A thin elastic strap can hold a pouch which hangs over the groin. This method is both comfortable and convenient, although a little embarrassing to use at times.

The Japanese use a *hadamaki,* a stomach sweater (Figure 7.4) to carry money and other flat valuables. The French have the same thing. The hadamaki would be useful to an American, since it would not be suspected by a thief. Jackets offer a wide range of possibilities. The heavier the jacket is,

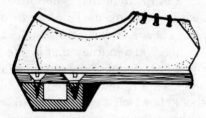

Figure 7.2. Hollow shoe heel.

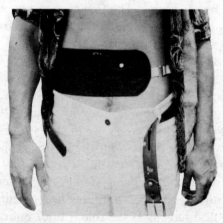

Figure 7.3. Money belts come in a variety of styles, including waist belts for under the shirt and leather belts with zippered compartments.

the more room is available for caches. Sometimes simply a hidden pocket opposite the usual inside pocket of a sport coat would not be spotted (Figure 7.5). Sweatbands in hats often carry valuables. Figure 7.1 shows another possibility, a cap with a concealed flap inside.

Figure 7.4. Japanese hadamaki or stomach sweater (photos by Lynn Kellner).

Figure 7.5. A jacket pocket can be placed on the side opposite the usual location of a coat pocket.

Items often carried in daily use can be utilized, such as a hollowed-out walking cane (see Figures 7.6 and 7.7). Glasses with large-enough frames could be modified to have hollow places. Rings, bracelets, necklace lockets can be used. "Mad money" carriers like this were used by farmers' wives in this country to transport their egg money to the general store or clothiers.

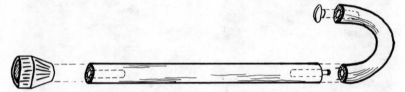

Figure 7.6. The hollow cane. An opening can be hidden under inlaid decorations as well.

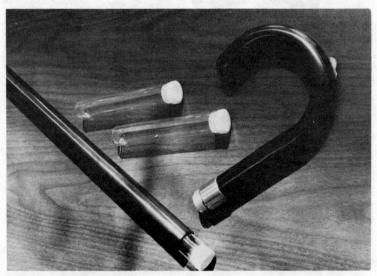

Figure 7.7. Other canes contain vials, swords, guns, rolled papers, and fishing poles!

PENS AND PENCILS

Pens and pencils are not likely to be stolen, and if they do work, they are less likely to be confiscated. Here are a few ways to accomplish this.

Pencil

Obtain two identical pencils. Remove the metal band and eraser from one, in any way necessary, but without scratching or breaking the pencil. Break the other pencil below the band and carefully gouge out the wood inside with a small screwdriver or an awl. On the first pencil, notice where holes were punched through the band and into the wood to hold it on. These are the key: carefully cut small grooves from the punched holes to the end of the pencil and a short groove off to one side (Figure 7.8). Then the band can be slipped on and slightly turned to keep it on tightly. Now drill a hole in the pencil that will be covered by the eraser and band; here you can conceal small treasures. A pencil-type ball pen that has an eraser can be prepared in the same way by cutting grooves in the plastic pen.

Non-button Ballpoints

Pull out the ink filler with pliers, cut it shorter, and replace it in the pen (Figure 7.9). Take the button off the other end, drlll a hole into the pen, and wrap tape around the button to keep it snug in the larger hole.

Cartridge Fountain Pen

Obtain two empty cartridges. Cut one short; then cut the end off the other, and glue it into the shortened tube (Figure 7.10). Fill the cartridge with ink and reassemble the working pen, in which you can now hide a small object.

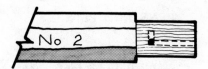

Figure 7.8. Locking groove to hold eraser on pencil.

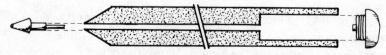

Figure 7.9. Hollow ballpoint pen.

Figure 7.10. Shortened cartridge for fountain pens.

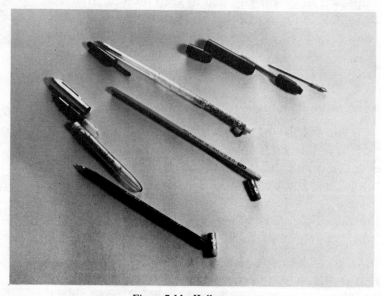

Figure 7.11. Hollow pens.

Tourists are expected to have cameras around their necks—but the film cartridge in the camera can have cash slipped inside, especially if you cut off part of the film to make more room in the cartridge.

Figure 7.12. Film cartridges are a useful cache for cash.

CLOTHING AND JEWELRY

Nearly everyone wears a wrist watch, and, since watches sometimes do not give the correct time, a nonfunctioning watch will not stand out. The back of a watch may be held on by several means; some are held by a tight gasket, some by threads. Once a watch is opened, perhaps by a watchmaker, disassembly is rather simple. Using a very small screwdriver, remove the innards. Reassemble by carefully gluing the hands on the inside of the face, so that the glue does not show from the outside. Glue the face to the glass; and glue the knob inside the case. (Solder is stronger than contact cement and longer lasting.) The back can be altered for easy access; just be sure it will not pop off unexpectedly. The watchband can also be a miniature money belt (Figure 7.13).

Hats are used as much for security storage as they are for shade or warmth! Tales abound of safe stash sombreros and stovepipe hats. Any high hat is easy to use, with cash in the sweatband or in a wallet or tobacco pouch strapped to the inside. Caps are less often used; they have usable sweatbands, but their floppiness makes them less secure than a rigid hat. A radial cap could be radially lined, with one section fastened with snaps or velcro. A lined cap could simply have one stitch slightly loosened, so that thin matter can be slipped in.

A hidden necklace could be worn under the neck fold of a thick knit sweater.

Hollow rings can be purchased from jewelers or antique dealers. They have long been used and are carefully treated by owners; so very old rings can be found intact. Bracelets, earrings, necklaces, and pendants are also used for love messages, poison, perfume, and diplomatic messages. A fancy

Figure 7.13. Watch band or wrist strap doubles as money belt (see Appendix A).

belt buckle can be worn by men without attracting attention (Figure 7.14).

In shoes, the hollow heel is a well-used screen, as we mentioned. Police officers can purchase radio transmitters built into a hollow heel. The liner of a shoe can be removed and slit. Cash can be slipped in and the thin pieces glued together to make detection impossible. The sole itself on some shoes can be gouged out from inside and the liner placed back on top.

Other devices akin to the money belt can be bought or fairly easily made. These include: the slingpoke (Figures 7.15, *left* and *right*), which fits under the arm and can be sewn up from easily available materials; and the leg-carrier and pocket sock, which enable one to use the loose space between leg and pants (Figure 7.16).

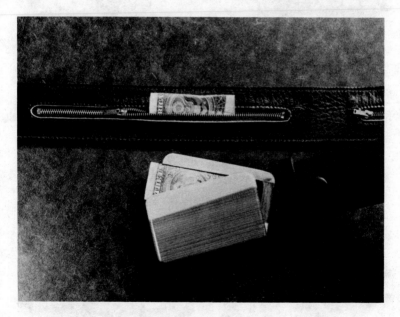

Figure 7.14. A moneybelt and a hollow belt buckle (see Appendix A).

Figure 7.15. *Left:* The sling-poke, a hidden shoulder harness. *Right:* The sling-poke as worn.

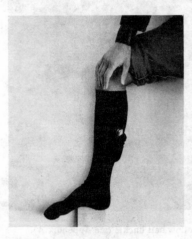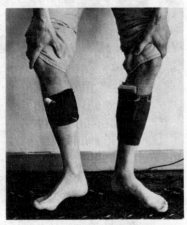

Figure 7.16. Leg-carriers (Leg Cache and Komfort Karrier) on right, and pocket sock on left (see Appendix A).

Finally, as a caution to any readers who are planning to travel, I offer Figure 7.17, which shows items confiscated by U.S. Customs agents. These include:

smuggler's vest, with hidden zippered pockets, and the
    bottom of the vest filled with hidden goods;
child's toy stuffed with contraband;
suitcase with false bottom;
book with some pages cut out;
soap bar hollowed out and waxed back up;
record album with baggie taped flat to record;
tampon with contraband taped on;

Figure 7.17. Confiscated contraband display courtesy of U.S. Customs.

cigarette case with hollow bottom;

medal case with goods inside top or bottom;

half a rubber ball used by a woman to pretend she was
pregant;

tin can (label removed, cut in half, resoldered, relabeled);

cardboard inserted in package that was cut out inside;

toothpaste tube, opened from bottom, and with goods
inserted into it;

books, with goods taped to inside of spine;

shoe polish can with hollow bottom;

medallion board, cut out under medallion;

sailor's bag with hidden pockets sewn inside;

deodorant powder container.

Remember, a customs agent is good at thinking of hiding
places; it's his job, and he probably enjoys it. You need to be
better than he is to fool him—and that's not easy.

Hiding Places on the Body

In hatband

In women's hair barrettes

In false caps on teeth

Swallowed with string tied
to teeth

Under false teeth

Loose in mouth

In processed hair, hairbuns
and wigs

In ears

Taped behind ears

In glass eyes

In nose

In hearing-aid glasses

In earrings

In hats

In military cap insignia

In lapel and shoulder patches

Behind campaign ribbons
and uniform brass

In love beads

In battery box of hearing aid

In fountain pens

In cuff links

In lining of clothing

In rings

Inside neck and wrist lockets,
bracelets, and charms

Inside ID bracelet

In casts

In false buttons

Taped under breast and
brassiere

In lapel of jackets and coats

In collar of shirts, jackets, and
coats

Hiding Places on the Body (Cont.)

Inside back of watch
In pockets
In eyeglass case
In contact-lens case
In false limbs
Under bandaids and bandages
In corsets
In rectum
In vagina
In cheeks of buttocks
In tie knot of tie and hand-
    kerchiefs
In jock straps
In wallet
In foreskin of penis
In belt buckles
In slit belts or zippered belts
Inside fly flap of trousers
Pinned to shorts
In swimming trunks
In male or female girdle
In cuffs and waistbands

In socks and shoes
In baby's diapers
In lipstick tube
In tobacco tins and pouches
In cigarette package
In cigarette lighter
In pill vials
Inside sanitary napkins or
    tampons
In 35-mm film cans
In inhalers
In compact
In cigarette filters
In gum sticks
Inside hollowed-out crutches
In hollow end of cane or
    umbrella
Inside feces bag
In thermos jugs
In canteens
In addressed envelopes
In liners of luggage

Figure 8.1.

Trove Transport

A trove of treasure occasionally has to be moved in a vehicle: car, bicycle, motorcycle, trailer, etc. The space in a vehicle that can be used for hiding is rather less than that in a house. Learning to make full use of limited space can be an excellent exercise. Since vehicles are mass-produced, they are more alike than most buildings, and any modifications will show unless they are perfectly constructed.

Any car will have a wide range of usable hiding places that require little if any construction. Beyond these, to have a usable scheme, the specific vehicle will need to be considered: its age and type of use, what will be hidden, how big it is, how fragile or noisy, who the treasure is being hidden from, how often access will be needed. If access will only be needed once, then greater care can be taken in construction of the compartment. If frequent access is necessary, a different plan will be more appropriate, one that takes inquisitive fingers and weather into account.

If an item sits in plain view on the seat, a passerby may take this as an invitation. To secrete is to dissuade. As a temporary barrier, the trunk removes an inviting article from view. The spaces under the front and rear seats, and the glove compartment, will be easy to use with little effort. Many cars have suitable temporary stash spots elsewhere, some known only to the hider.

To move into more complex hiding, view the car for possibilities that require a little more effort. Headlights or rear lights are often enclosed in a protective case. Metal bumper guards or even bumpers could be used. Hub caps could also be used for a short-term haul, with the items carefully bundled inside soft cloth. The inside of fenders or the body may not be suspected by a grabber. An interior door panel can sometimes be removed to supply a wall-type hollow. Some shift knobs are hollow. In certain seats, the inside can be reached by dexterous hands. A tape cassette could be modified, as can the space behind speakers or inside radios, heaters, or air conditioners. A broken radio or tape deck can be very empty. Removing an overhead lamp fixture could give access to the ceiling space. Armrests are occasionally vacant. Consoles are often used (and often suspected). Wealth can be stored inside the tube or between the tire and tube in the spare tire.

Additional possibilities range from a magnetic keycase to major revisions in body work. Vans often use cloth sun screens to give some visual privacy. An auxiliary gas tank can be added for goods more precious than gasoline. A steering wheel can be wrapped with money, then have a cover laced over it. A faulty tachometer or other instrument offers untenanted room. A secret compartment can be welded somewhere under the chassis if you have the skill or know a trustworthy craftsperson.

A motorcycle? Even more challenging! Registration slips are often hidden inside the handlebars. The headlight case is used to carry spare bulbs and fuses. The gas tank could contain a well-wrapped package. Wires are strung through the frame. Instruments have hollow bottoms to allow room for the light bulbs, which slip into small holes. A careful placement within the air-filter box can serve for short runs. The far inside of a footpeg rubber can be filled. The tire-tube trick could again be used. Many seats have air holes in the bottom or can be reupholstered for longer storage. Some motorcycles can be run without a working battery. Inside the wheel hubs some space is available. Where else? Don't overdo it. If all these spots were filled with gold, it would double the weight of the motorcycle!

What about a bicycle? Access to a bicycle frame is easier than access to a motorcycle frame. Handlebars can again be filled. Inside mounted reflectors is an empty hole. Front tubes are usually uninhabited. The long-distance traveler and the biggest smugglers do not usually travel by bicycle, but bicycles still offer potential.

House trailers, campers, mobile homes, motorhomes are fascinating blends of house and car. Frame construction is often similar to that in houses, but uses thinner and less bulky walls. Many of the techniques used for walls can be adapted to the trailer, as can those for cars. Even well-designed trailers leave untouched spaces to the imagination of the traveler. The thicker bathroom wall can have a secret door that opens onto shelves placed among the pipes. A *set-in* box can be used here. Once again, breaking the usual habit routines can place the searcher at a disadvantage. An unscrewed light fixture can open the thin roof space for use. The structure that supports fold-up beds can provide unconsidered potentials. Space under the floor in some units could be adapted to hiding, depending on the construction of the floor. One can adapt the techniques used with a chest of drawers to the built-in drawers in a trailer. Air and water heaters, air conditioners, pumps,

Figure 8.2. Mobil home: secret cache under boards under mattress.

water storage, and sewage tanks are all fitted into their space
as tightly as possible; yet all leave ample room for construction
of a hiding place. Travel safely!

> The care we give our valued goods
> Protects them from envisioned hoods;
> So once you've got the odds well beat,
> Stand back, and admire your feat!

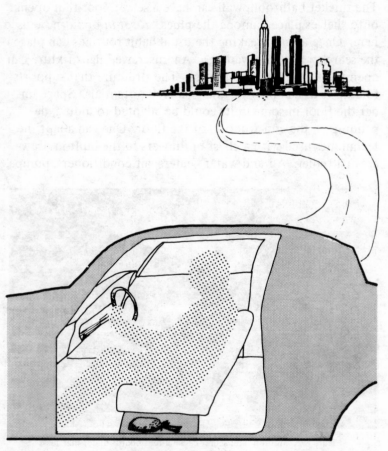

Figure 8.3.

Hiding Places in an Automobile

Inside horn
In air filter
In false heater hoses
In heater
In false battery
In oil filter
In windshield-washer bag
In carburetor
Inside oil cap
In false dual muffler
In hollow voltage regulator
On top of gas tank (suspended or concealed in compartment)
In 35-mm film cans
In rocker panels
Tied to axle
On underside of fender
In tail pipe
In insulation under hood
Under chrome
Behind Volkswagen battery box
Inside trunk lids
Inside tubing on roof racks
Inside tubing on surfboard or ski rack
Under tire air-valve caps
Taped behind bumper
In antenna base
Taped to rolled-down window
In license-plate holder
In frame
In headlights and taillights
In hub caps
In picnic jug in trunk
Inside double roof (which surplus police cars have)
In spare-tire treads and well
In convertible tops

In trunk
In fusebox
In false bottom of trunk beds
In cigarette lighter
Under floorboard
Under seats
Inside back seat
In vents (air and heater)
In glove compartment: on top of compartment or behind trap door
In radio-speaker grill
Inside shift knobs
Inside steering column
In dome light
In and under ashtrays
In key case
In service-station travel kits
Under brake and gas pedals
Inside sun visors
Under carpet
Inside false radio
In hide-a-key
In pill vials
Under floor mats
Inside upholstery
Inside instrument panel and ornamental objects on dashboard
In compartments under floor of older VW's
Inside floor consoles
Inside dash knobs
In arm rest
Inside flashlight
Inside toolbox
Inside light sockets

Hiding Places in Motorcycles

In tail lights
Under seat
Inside handlebar tubing
Inside battery box
In tool box
Rolled up inside sleeping bag
   or other item carried
In concealed compartment in
   custom gas tank

Inside lining of motorcycle
   helmet
In concealed pockets in padded
   clothing
Behind headlight
Behind instrument gauges
Inside tires

Figure 9.1.

The Secret Life
(Or, How to Live
With Your Hiding Place)

Have you now built a hiding place? Does this secret spot need special care? Yes, indeed it does! Unless you intend to display your secrets to all thrill seekers, *KEEP IT HIDDEN!* The moment friends or relations discover or are shown *one* hiding place, then the question will always float in their minds: what else is hidden, and where, and how? Their curious fingers will explore every chair they sit in, every door they go through, every wall in the house. Their eager eyes will constantly float throughout their visit, their minds titillated in wonder. Is there a safe behind that painting? How does this bookcase open? Is all the molding really attached? Why is the bathroom being repainted and new tile being put on the floor? There *must* be a secret room behind that . . ..

To live successfully with your hiding place as part of your private life, watch yourself. Stay aware of the desire to show off the work, to take pride in the craftsmanship, the cleverness, and all the treasure within, bedded safely from perusal. Do you feel guilty about having a place more secure than anyone you know? DO NOT TELL THEM. If you must, leave this book lying around your house when friends are coming. If they ask about it, say you have thought about building a secret place and ask what they think of this idea. This will alert them to the possibility and share it with them, and yet keep your *own* place the secret it should be forever!

Do not let your pride gallop over your judgment! Not even your children should know. But they probably will; their crystal-clear observations, although unintentional, can reveal the concealed chamber. If you use the place frequently, it is easy to get into the habit of automatically going to it. Be careful not to use it out of habit while someone else is

111

with you. And *never* leave a sandwich hidden: a dog will nose it out very quickly and wag the children to the spot! No amount of explaining will cure their curiosity until they see the real reason for the dog's actions.

Keep in mind concept/construction/context, and use *context* not only for construction, but socially as well. Your own actions will draw upon your skill not to reveal your hidden place. It will test your ability to personally screen and misdirect attention that could be focused upon your secret. Once the stash is built, only then does the biggest challenge start! Remember: the security is breached when *one* other person knows about it; so beware!

> Beware the inner need
> To share the cloistered deed;
> Take the warning, and take heed,
> To keep the secret safe from greed!

Appendix A

Sources for Hiding Devices

Electric outlet box
    (Figure 5.5):

Invisible Wall Safe
    The Maurice A. Kimball Company,
        Inc.
    Security Products Division
    1926 South Pacific Coast Highway,
        #228
    Redondo Beach, Calif. 90277

Soss hinges (Figure 6.5):   Available at hardware stores.

Key holder (Figure 6.28):   Available at locksmiths, hardware, and
    auto-parts stores.

Magna-Stash (Figure 6.28):   Brother Bob Productions
    Post Office Box 1868
    Hollywood, Calif. 90068

Soda can with screw-top
    lid (Figure 6.28):   Collector's Items, Ltd.
    Post Office Box 386
    Cardiff, Calif. 92007

Mini-soda bottle (Figure 6.28):   Cathi and Roy's Favorite Toys
    Post Office Box 30512
    Seattle, Wash. 98103

Hollow cane (Figure 7.6):   Pioneer Company
    110 West Washington St.
    Lisbon, Ohio 44432

Money belts (Figure 7.3):   Custom made belts and shoe liners:
    Western Manufacturing Company,
        Inc.
    149 Ninth St.
    San Francisco, Calif. 94103

Hollow belt buckle
(Figure 7.14):   Chuckle buckle
                                  (High)^2 Enterprises
                                  Post Office Box 11135
                                  Alexandria, Virginia 22312

Watch band (Figure 7.13):   The Pleasure Chest Sales, Ltd.
                                  120 11th Ave.
                                  New York, N.Y. 10011

Pocket Socks (Figure 7.16):   Keepers Industries, Inc.
                                  6415 Desoto Ave.
                                  Woodland Hills, Calif. 91364

Komfort Karrier (Figure 7.16):   Komfort Karrier, Inc.
                                  Post Office Box 638
                                  Turlock, Calif. 95380

Leg Cache (Figure 7.16):   Mackenzie Company
                                  Post Office Box 29
                                  Calabasas, Calif. 91302

Glossary

Contact boat. Carriers of alcohol who waited outside the territorial limits.

Grabber burglar. A grab-and-run burglar, who has low skills and goes for quick hits.

Hadamaki. Japanese stomach sweater, used to conceal valuables.

Ham. Six bottles of alcohol banded together during the Civil War.

Hidden. An object that is secreted from view.

Hiding. Consciously concealing an object for shelter or protection.

Inpo. The art of hiding in Japanese.

Kura. Japanese treasure house.

Mezuzah. A small case placed on doorways by Jews with verses from the Torah placed inside.

Misdirection. Redirecting the searcher's mind away from the sought object.

Ninja. Japanese spies during the thirteenth to seventeenth centuries; they carried on a tradition somewhat analogous to that of the Western gunslinger.

Professional burglar. A skilled burglar who steals what and when he can.

Screen. To hide an object from view.

Selector burglar. The most skilled burglar, who chooses specific objects to steal.

Stash. To hide in a secret place.

Trapping. Secret compartments in the bottom of a boat.

Underground Railroad. The group that smuggled slaves out of the southern United States prior to the Civil War.

Bibliography

General

Krotz, David, *How to Hide Almost Anything*. New York: Morrow, 1975. An excellent exposition of low-energy, high-risk hiding places.

Poe, Edgar Allan, *The Purloined Letter*. For a short story, Poe provides a wealth of ideas as well as a dissertation on the psychology of hiding.

History

Adams, Andrew, *Ninja: The Invisible Assassins*. Burbank, Calif.: Ohara Publications, 1976. History and effects of the ninja.

Barry, James P., *The Noble Experiment, 1919–1933*. New York: Franklin Watts, 1972. A short, concise, and clear statement about prohibition, its causes, effects, and legacies.

Berteaut, Simone, *Piaf*. New York: Dell, 1973. Edith Piaf's life is shared by her sister, who lived much of it with her.

Fea, Allan, *Secret Chambers and Hiding Places*. London: Bousfield, 1901. An exciting and thorough rummage through many hiding places in England, with a full chapter on Nicholas Owen, and several about the hidden priests!

Frank, Anne, *Diary of a Young Girl*. New York: Doubleday, 1952. A young Jewish girl passes her thirteenth through fourteenth years in a hidden room in occupied Holland.

Gara, Larry, *The Liberty Line: The Legend of the Underground Railroad*. University of Kentucky Press, 1961. A clear separation between fact and fancy on this fascinating subject.

Gerard, John, *The Autobiography of a Hunted Priest*. New York: Pellegrini & Cudahy, 1952. A stunning account of the times that bred Nicholas Owen's skills.

Squiers, Granville, *Secret Hiding Places*. 1934. Tower, 1971. An expanded look at the British hiding places which goes beyond Fea's enchanting tales. One chapter on "Hints for Searchers."

ten Boom, Corrie, *The Hiding Place*. Minneapolis, Minn.: World Wide Pictures, 1971. A heart-felt story by a member of the Dutch underground during World War II.

Waters, Harold, *Smugglers of Spirits*. New York: Hastings House, 1971. A personal account of the Rum War by a retired officer of the Coast Guard.

Burglars' View

Barnes, Robert Earl, *Are You Safe from Burglars?* New York: Doubleday, 1971. Barnes was a professional burglar for twenty years, and shares his experiences as a way to help occupants protect their valuables. Most of the advice is concerned with preventing entry; one chapter is on hiding places.

Munro, Andrew Keith, *Autobiography of a Thief*. London: Michael Joseph, 1972. A detailed transition between grabber and professional.

Finding Hiding Places

Packard, Vance, *The Hidden Persuaders.* New York: Simon and Schuster, 1966.
A look at how modern marketers use an understanding of the human mind to
secretly tempt the purchasers' decisions.

Art of Hiding People

Doyle, Sir Arthur Conan, *The Complete Sherlock Holmes.* New York: Doubleday,
n.d. The master-finder shares his methods.

Fantasy

Norton, Mary, *The Borrowers.* New York: Harcourt, Brace, 1952. Ever wondered
about your missing things, like thimbles, hatpins, etc.? Ever thought they
might have been borrowed by someone?
Thurber, James, *The Secret Life of Walter Mitty.* Mitty lives the adventures within.
Wells, H.G., *The Invisible Man.* What is it like to live without a body? The invisible man quickly finds out!

Other

Ladd, Richard S., *A Descriptive List of Treasure Maps and Charts.* Library of
Congress, Map Division, Washington, D.C., 1964; LCC: 64-60033. A list of
treasure maps in The Library of Congress and how to obtain copies.
Wolfe, James Raymond, *Secret Writing.* New York: McGraw-Hill, 1970. Cryptog-
raphy put forth and explained so we can all use it.

Index

Author Biography

Peter Hjersman: here is a man _____ who is a builder.

He builds with words, lines and form, spirit, soul and heart.

He writes about building–*Dome Notes,* an exploration of alternative structures, and about growing–*Light Growth,* poems of transition. (These are available through Erewon Press, P.O. Box 4253, Berkeley, CA 94704).